Contents

Acknowledgements

p. 25: extracts from the English translation of
The Roman Missal © 1973, ICEL. All rights reserved.
p. 25: English translation of the Gloria, Creed by the
International Consultation on English Texts (ICET).
p. 44 and 45: Sikh Missionary Society

Cover photo: Andes Press Agency

Photo Credits: p. 5: Sally and Richard Greenhill;
p.9: Andes Press Agency; p. 10: (bottom) Andes
Press Agency; p. 11: Andes Press Agency; Ronald
Sheridan; p. 12: (top) Oxford Mail and Times;
(others) Andes Press Agency; p. 14: Sally and Richard
Greenhill; p. 17: Sally and Richard Greenhill;
p. 18: J. Allan Cash; p. 19: Andes Press Agency;
p. 20: Andes Press Agency; p. 23: Sally and Richard
Greenhill; p. 25: Andes Press Agency; p. 31: (left
top and bottom) Sally and Richard Greenhill; (right)
Hutchison Library; p. 34: Andes Press Agency;
p. 40: J. Allan Cash; p. 42: David Richardson;
p. 43: David Richardson; p. 46: Andes Press
Agency; p. 47: Andes Press Agency; p. 49: Andes
Press Agency; p. 50: Andes Press Agency;
p. 58: Sally and Richard Greenhill; p. 60: Sally and
Richard Greenhill; p. 67: Xinhua News Agency;
p. 68: David Richardson; p. 72: Andes Press Agency

Weaving the Web

Communication
Celebration·Values

Level 1

A modular programme of Religious Education

Richard Lohan and Mary McClure SND

Collins

Collins Liturgical Publications
8 Grafton Street, London W1X 3LA

Collins Liturgical in Canada
Novalis, Box 9700, Terminal
375 Rideau St, Ottawa, Ontario K1G 4B4

Collins Dove
PO Box 316, Blackburn, Victoria 3130

Collins Liturgical New Zealand
PO Box 1, Auckland

First published 1989
© 1989 Richard Lohan and Mary McClure

Programme Components

Community, Story, People

Level One	0 00 599149 8
Level Two	0 00 599150 1
Level Three	0 00 599151 X

Communication, Celebration, Values

Level One	0 00 599152 8
Level Two	0 00 599153 6
Level Three	0 00 599154 4

Teacher's Book   0 00 599156 0

The National Project of Catechesis and Religious Education
Published with the authority of the Department for Christian Doctrine and Formation of the Bishop's Conference of England and Wales

Nihil obstat   Father Anton Cowan, *censor*
Imprimatur   Rt. Rev. John Crowley, V.G.,
          Bishop in Central London
Westminster, 8th May, 1989
The Nihil obstat and Imprimatur are a declaration that a book or pamphlet is considered to be free from doctrinal or moral error. It is not implied that those who have granted the Nihil obstat and Imprimatur agree with the contents, opinions or statements expressed.

Typographical design and typesetting by
VAP Publishing Services, Kidlington, Oxon.
Illustrations by Clyde Pearson
Printed by Bell and Bain Ltd, Glasgow

This continues the work you have begun in
Religious Education.

The course as a whole is called
WEAVING THE WEB

WEAVING THE WEB is an R.E. programme in which you are invited to take an active part. Like a weaver criss-crossing threads to make cloth, you will be picking up and linking together the four main strands or contexts of your experience of community life –

Decide in which of the four areas you might be exploring

a religious group

your school community

young people in a third world setting

getting on with parents

Write these four examples in your workbook and put the appropriate symbol next to each.

Family community

Local community

Plural community

Global community

Every half-term or so, you will be studying a short unit of work (a module). Each module has *Tasks* for you to do, including ways that can help you to work out what progress you are making.

Please remember . . . each module is designed to be a basic guide for your work.

The modules do not contain everything you need to know and understand and experience in R.E.

The modules are a springboard for what you and your class will be involved in, with the guidance and support of your teachers.

All the modules are called after important aspects of life and of religion. Like the spider's web that catches everything that comes its way, religious education has to do with all aspects of life and of religion.

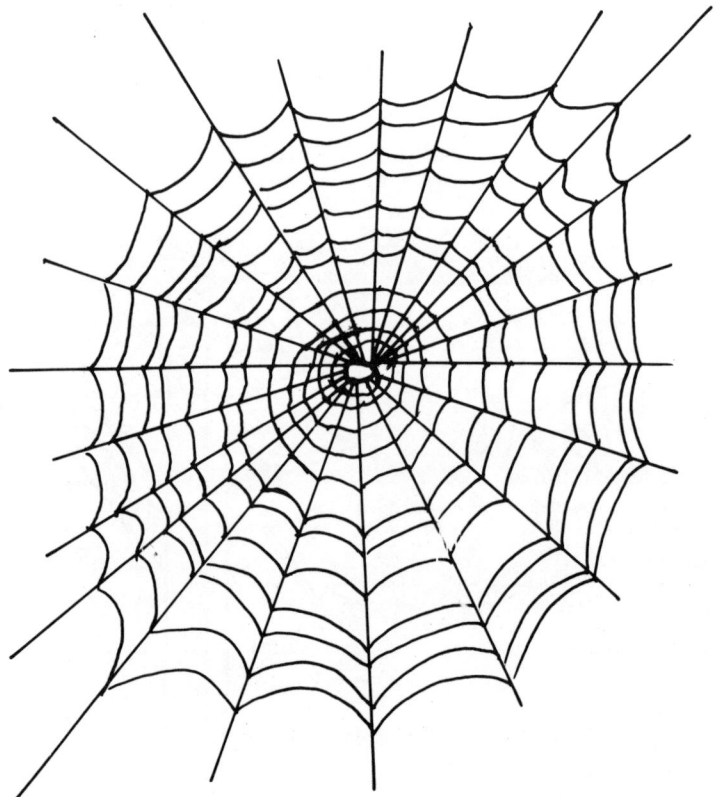

You are starting a Level One module of your R.E. programme *Weaving the Web*.

This module of work is called

Communication

It is all about how people communicate with each other, and how people in the main religious traditions communicate with and respond to the mystery at the centre of their lives, through prayer and worship.

Here are some of the things you will be doing in this module:

- **exploring** your experience of various ways of communicating.

- **exploring** how people use words, gestures, signs as symbols to communicate.

- **describing** how people communicate and respond to each other in your family and local community.

- **reflecting** on how people keep in touch with others, with themselves, with the natural world, and with mystery.

- **exploring** a Christian symbol in a global context.

- **discovering** and **discussing** some main elements in Hindu worship.

- **examining** and **comparing** some forms of Christian worship.

- **finding out** how Christians pray.

- **exploring** the Our Father.

- **exploring** your own experience of prayer and worship.

Exploring communication

In the first part of this module, you will be exploring how people communicate, including your own experience of communication with your friends, in your family and in your local community.

Communication is about keeping in touch. Let's explore the ways we keep in touch with others.

Communication usually involves some or all of these:

- making contact with people
- keeping in touch with people
- spending time together
- sharing an activity
- letting people know how you think or feel
- talking and listening
- writing/expressing/performing

Task 1

Draw these hands into your workbook. Have you ever noticed the way some people talk with their hands?

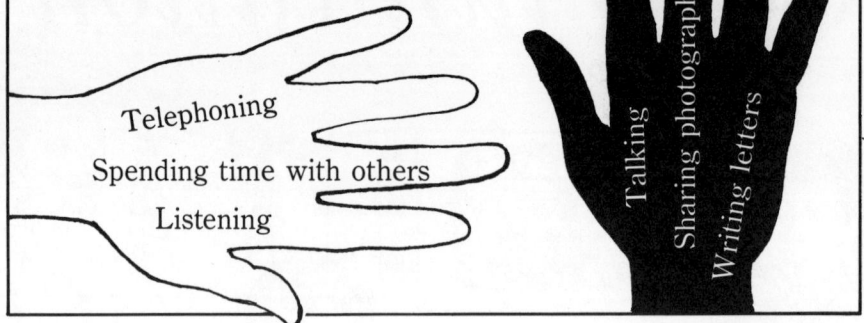

Telephoning

Spending time with others

Listening

Talking

Sharing photographs

Writing letters

Extension work

A

Do you talk a lot?

Do you enjoy communicating with others?

B

Have you ever written or received a letter which, for you, was an important letter? Why was the letter important for you? *Write* about it!

Communication profile

Task 2

Think of yourself in the course of an average day or week. Try to calculate how much of your time is spent communicating with others.

Make a profile chart like the one on the next page and fill it in, estimating in minutes and hours the time spent communicating with different people/things.

Look back at what has been written above about the activities which are usually involved in communicating.

Estimate what proportion of your waking hours is spent communicating.

Compare your chart with a friend's.

Find an effective way of communicating your findings with the rest of your class.

	FRIENDS	FAMILY	OTHERS	ANIMALS	MEDIA (Books, papers, TV, records)
ME					

Extension work

A

Look again at the list in Task 1 of what communication usually involves. Now *think* if there are any times in the day or week when you are not communicating with anybody at all.

B

Reflection

Can you think of any situation where choosing not to communicate is a way of getting a message across?

Role-play some situations of this sort: e.g. After an argument at home, I lock myself in my room.

Ways of communicating

Task 3

gesture   words   sound

dance   life-style   sculpture

picture   sign   taking action doing something

Louise is very happy indeed. Martin is extremely worried. Janine wants to protest about the danger to seals from pollution.

GROUP WORK

Explore together how Louise, Martin and Janine might communicate feelings or ideas through some of the ways mentioned above.

Extension work

A

Find out and *display* some examples of how people use these various forms of communication.

B

Consider which of these forms of communication you yourself have used or are using now to express what you think or feel.

Let's look more closely at each of these ways of communicating.

Language

Perhaps this is the first form of communication which comes to mind, although it is not the first way of communicating that most of us learn.

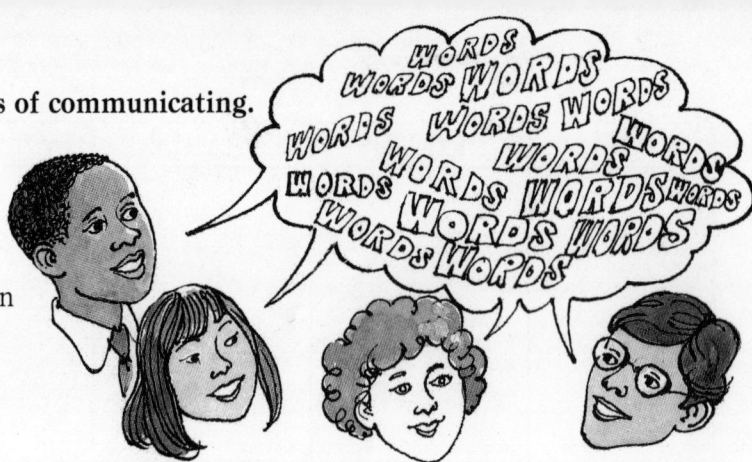

Task 4

Explore language as a form of communication in the community.

Can you answer these questions . . .

. . . about you as an individual

1. What language or languages do you speak and understand?

2. How did you come to learn the language or languages you speak?

3. What language or languages do or did your grandparents speak?

4. How many languages are there in which you know at least a couple of words: e.g. *glasnost, adios amigos, pizzeria . . .* Write down the name of the language and then a couple of words from it.

5. Do a neighbourhood watch – *make a list* of all the words from languages other than English which are now in common use on signs in your area: e.g. *kebab . .*

6. Is there a language which you wish you could speak? Say why.

. . . about your school

7. How many languages are spoken by members of your class? You will have to find a way of communicating the answer to question 1 in order to work this out.

8. How many languages are spoken by members of your school?

9. Are there any special words or meanings used in your class or among your friends which nobody else uses or knows about? Make a list of these.

. . . about your local community

10. What languages are commonly spoken in your locality? How does the way people speak in your community differ from elsewhere in the country? Are there special words or accents used here that are not used elsewhere?

11. Do you think it is important that everyone in your community should have the opportunity to learn the most commonly spoken language of the country?

12. What is done in your community to help groups preserve their own forms of language and communicate them to their children?

. . . about languages throughout the world

13. Roughly how many languages are spoken throughout the world, do you think? Where would you find this information? Perhaps you could do this for homework.

14. What do you think are the good points about a world where people speak many different languages?

15. Do you think the languages spoken throughout the world are basically very similar or basically very different? How could you find this out?

Extension work

A

Make a display with a word or words from as many different languages as you can. *Label* each one with the language it comes from.

B

Learn the alphabet from a language that uses a way of writing different from your own family language. *Write* your name in it.

αδвг   ﺣﻴﺤﻰ

αβγδ   אבג

Communicating with words

Task 5

1. Here are some of the ways that words are used in communication.

ha! ha!

a Letter

A story . . .

RULES

MANIFESTO
Promises, promises . . .

INSTRUCTIONS
1 . . . .
2 . . . .
3 . . . .

SARCASM

Proverbs

oral history

♪ lyrics

𝆕 a poem . . .

A WARNING

hurtful criticism

Find examples of words used in some of these ways, and write them down.
See if you can add to this list of ways of communicating; find examples to go with your new entries.

2. Do you know anyone who uses words particularly effectively or powerfully? Can you explain why? It could be someone you know (e.g. a teacher) or it could be a politician or someone you see on television.

Extension work

A

Make two columns, headed *Spoken word/Written word*. Divide your list between them. Will any entries appear in both columns?

B

WORD GAME

Explore in a thesaurus or by brainstorming, phrases using the word 'word' or 'words', and explain what they mean:
for example, to start you off:
'empty words'
'my word is my bond'

Thesaurus: a book containing words grouped by their meanings.

Communicating without words

Not all communication uses words.

One form of communication without using words is called 'body language'. Body language is non-verbal communication.

Task 6

> **Non-verbal** means without words.

1. Look at the people below and describe what each person is telling us.

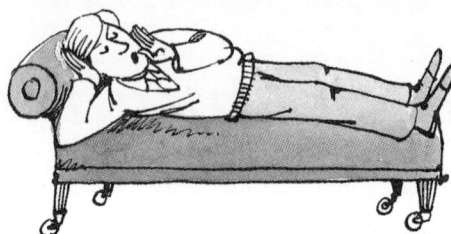

Now, you try saying the same things without words. Did you use the same actions and have the same expressions on your face?

2. Look at the gestures below. What are they communicating?

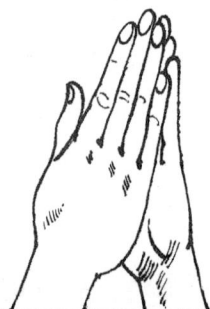

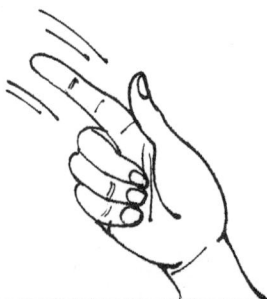

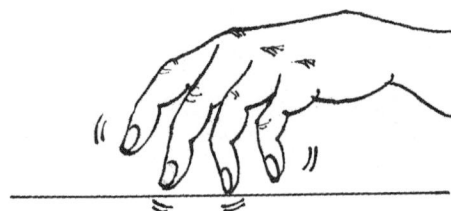

Extension work: a group activity

A and **B**

As a group, *devise* body language to express the following emotions:

frustration	satisfaction	anger	fear	excitement
annoyance	boredom	protest	delight	triumph

and/or

choose one person to use body language/posture/gesture/movement/expression to *communicate* a feeling: the group is to *guess* what the feeling is.

Understanding non-verbal communication

Most people are very skilled at understanding what is communicated without words, in the shapes, expressions and gestures people use. Very often, this form of communication is more effective than using words.

Task 7

Roleplay the following

Someone is very ill, a neighbour telephones the emergency services, but is too shocked to give the correct details. You are passing by . . .

or

You have lost your voice. You have to give an important message to someone at home. You cannot write as you have twisted your writing hand at P.E.

Write about how you felt during the role-play – was it frustrating, fun, frightening . . . etc.

Extension work

A

Write a short story using a mixture of words and sketches of facial expressions e.g. "When Jo got out of bed that morning he felt

but when he remembered it was Wednesday and P.E. he felt

B

Sometimes people say one thing to us in words, while we can see that their whole self is telling us something quite different:

for example, when Mum says, 'No, I'm not worried really. It's all right', but we can see that her brow is furrowed and she is clenching her hands . . .

or

when Grandad says, 'I feel fine', yet every time he moves we can see that his arthritis is very painful . . .

Describe an experience you have had where words were belied by body signs.

(You may need your teacher to explain what 'belied' means).

ASSESS your work!

How did we do?

Tasks 1 – 7

1. *Name three different ways in which people communicate.*
2. *How many of the daytime hours do you spend communicating?*
3. *How many languages are present in your class room?*
4. *Do you remember any foreign words? What do they mean?*
5. *What is the difference between verbal and non-verbal communication?*
6. *How do people communicate feelings of happiness?*

Did you do any extension work? Which did you enjoy most?

In the tasks which follow, you will be learning about signs and symbols, and how they are used in worship.

Communicating through signs and symbols

Signs are usually an effective way of communicating, provided people know the meaning of the signs.

Task 8

Do you know what the following signs mean? Discuss each one with your partner, make a sketch of it in your workbook or file and then write in what you think the sign means.

Sign	Meaning	Your own sign for this
⚠	_____	
🚫	_____	
🚫	_____	
P	_____	

Extension work

A

Make a list of the signs you pass on your way from school to home.

Explain what they mean.

B

Look again at task 8: a number of quite different signs could have been used to get the same message across.

Design a new sign for each of these four, and *draw* it in beside your list of meanings.

Let's reflect on signs and symbols

Signs

Some signs do more than just give information. They become so closely connected with what they point to that they take on a deeper meaning, summing up or communicating what the real thing involves.

The Olympic logo is a symbol not just of the Olympic Games but of all the ideals which the Olympic movement tries to promote.

A national flag, a city's *coat of arms*, a school *badge* – all of these may be signs which are symbolic – all symbolize something of what it is to belong to or be part of that country, city, or school community.

Signs are made by people. They give information or point to the meaning of something.

Signs can be invented or changed.

This sign   has been replaced by   this sign

This sign   has been replaced by   this sign

BRITISH RAILWAYS

Symbols

We use *symbols* because they are closely linked or connected with what they stand for and they communicate a meaning or experience which is difficult to put into words.

Sometimes an everyday object is used as a symbol, to communicate something about the quality of a spiritual experience . . . an experience which is hard to describe in words.

Symbols are usually chosen because they have a close link with the meaning of the thing they represent. A symbol is less likely to change or to be changed.

For example **WATER** is a symbol of life in many cultures and faiths. Perhaps the main reason why water is used as a symbol of life is because of its importance in keeping people alive. Without water, we die.

The symbol of water communicates an important truth about living things, without using words.

Task 9

Food, fire, light are also symbols found in many cultures and faiths.

Choose one of these.

With your partner, write down all the 'meanings' you can find in your chosen symbol.

Share these with the class.

Extension work

A

A young man gives some presents to the woman he loves. They are:

a rose
a jewel
perfume
a ring
a locket with his photograph
  inside

What do you think these symbols communicate?

B

Symbols which remind us of the beauty of the world or of love or courage, loyalty, strength etc are often used by advertisers to sell their products:
e.g. diving off a cliff/swimming in a raging sea/climbing a high mountain . . . to deliver chocolates to the person you love!

This week, pay special attention to commercials and *make a list* of examples like these.

Reflect on the use of candles in worship

Worship uses many symbols.

For example, in many acts or ways of worshipping, candles are used.

- a candle which is lit in a special place for worship may remind the worshippers/believers that God is present.

- A candle may remind Christian worshippers that Jesus Christ said: 'I am the light of the world'.

> For people who believe in God, **worship** is a way of communicating with God, and rendering praise and thanks to the One who creates and sustains them. It is one of the ways in which they experience God relating to them.

In Christian worship, candles were first used when Christians had to act like a secret society and meet underground in what is now called the catacombs.

Find out why Christians had to go 'underground'.

Task 10

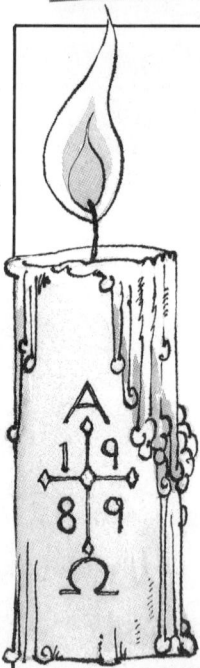

The Paschal Candle is a Christian symbol.

Describe what you see in the drawing of the Paschal Candle.

Find out what the signs on the Paschal Candle mean:

1. ◇◇◇◇◇ *(five pieces of incense): why are they used?*

2. *Why put a date on the candle?*

3. *Why use a cross?*

4. *What are* A *and* Ω *? What do they symbolise?*

> **Paschal:** to do with the Jewish Festival of Passover and the Christian Easter
>
> **The Paschal Candle** is sometimes called *The Easter Candle*

A   Ω

Extension work

A

Make or *draw* a Paschal Candle

B

Find out more about the use of candles in worship.

Christian symbols

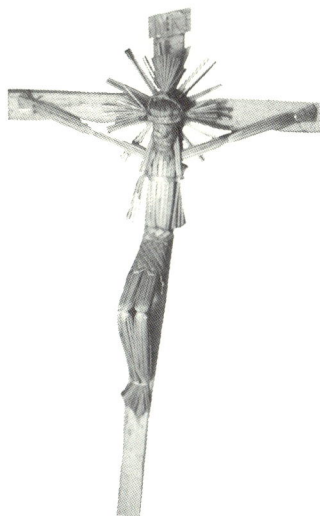

You have probably seen the Christian symbol called a crucifix: a crucifix is a cross with the figure of Jesus on it. It is especially familiar to Catholic Christians.

The crucifix is a symbol which communicates what Christians believe about the death and resurrection of Jesus Christ.

The crucifix is also a symbol of how much God loves the world:

'God so loved the world that he sent his only Son to die for our sins.'

Task 11

Christianity is a world religion: there are Christians in almost every country of the world.

Look at the illustrations on this page which show crucifixes from different countries of the world.

Write a sentence to say what each of these communicates to you.

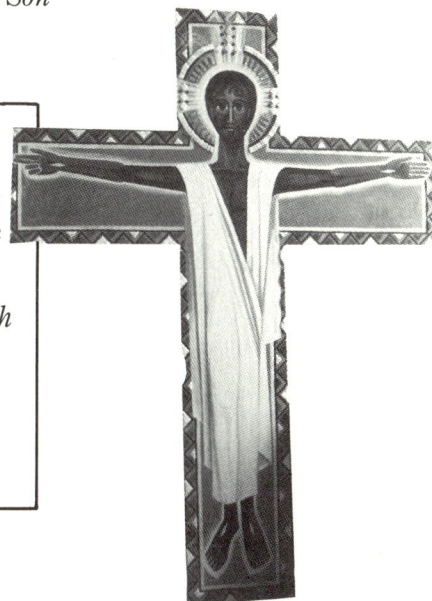

Extension work

A
Draw a crucifix and *write* under your drawing what you intend it to communicate.

B
Why do you think these crucifixes are different from each other?

Which do you find communicates to you the best? *Why?*

Exploring Christian worship

Worship is also a way of expressing what a person or a community believes about God and their relationship to God.

Worship can be the way a person responds to God's presence in his or her life.

Worship is also what happens at public or formal meetings of believers.

Worship is a dramatic or symbolic activity.

Look at the pictures of different forms of Christian worship.

They show

- a Meeting of a group of Friends – Quakers

- an Ukrainian Orthodox liturgy

- a Roman Catholic Mass with folk music

- a prayer meeting

- meditation

Match each description to one of the pictures.

Describe what you see in each picture.

Consider how the worshippers in each are communicating with God: don't forget words/ gestures/silence/symbols.

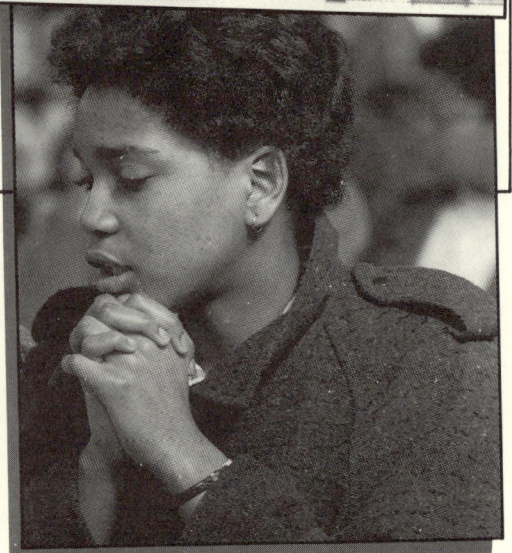

Extension work

A

How are the human senses used in these acts of worship? *List* each of the five senses, and then say how they are used?

B

If there is formal worship in school, do the following survey:

I think assemblies are...

When there is prayer or worship in school I feel......

If we could .... at assembly then ....

When we are together at assembly I find it easy/ difficult to ....

Sometimes during school prayer/worship I............

I think Mass at school is ....

ASSESS your work!

How did we do?

Tasks 8–12

1. *Can you explain what a sign is?*
2. *Give an example of a symbol and say why it is used as a symbol.*
3. *Did you learn anything new about Christian worship?*
4. *What did you find out about worship/assembly in your school from the survey?*
5. *Which tasks did you enjoy/not enjoy? How would you make the tasks more interesting?*

Exploring Hindu worship
Puja *Read Rakesh Pradhan's story ...*

Hello, my name is Rakesh. I'm 12 and I live in Liverpool. My family is Hindu. I like listening to Rick Astley and Kim Wilde and I support Everton. I go to the Community Comp. just around the corner from our house - I've only been there six months, but I really like it, especially the photography club. I've got my own camera, and I now know how to develop my own photographs.
A few weeks ago it was our class's turn to do an Assembly and Miss asked me and Jaynesh (one of my friends from Junior school) if we would help organise a small group of our class to do an Assembly about Puja-Hindu worship. When she used the proper word for Hindu worship, I was quite impressed. It's amazing how much teachers know!
Puja means any kind of Hindu worship.
Chris and Sue, two class friends were keen to join in so I asked them to look after objects, sound effects and smells! Actually they hadn't a clue about Hindu worship so I invited them to our house so that they could have a look at our home shrine.
I wanted the Assembly to be good so that others would understand something about my culture and our Hindu ways of worshipping.
My mum explained to them, that for Hindus worship is a whole way of life and that for us everything in life is for offering to God.
Every morning after we have washed and dressed, and before we have breakfast, we pray. One corner of our living room is set aside as a special shrine - we have a statue of Krishna, who is very young and handsome and is an incarnation of Vishnu.
Sue looked puzzled so mum explained that Hindus believe that God, <u>Brahman</u>, is in everything and is everywhere but appears in three forms, called <u>Brahma</u>, <u>Vishnu</u> and <u>Shiva</u>. These and many other gods make it easier for us to picture what God is like; they appear as humans and as animals. Chris spotted the elephant-headed god - <u>Ganesha</u> who is the son of <u>Shiva</u>. He is a symbol of strength and wisdom and is very popular among Hindu children.
In the morning, we light a candle next to the shrine and then we stand quietly with our eyes closed and our arms outstretched and say our prayers.
There are flowers and bright decorations near the shrine as an offering to God. We also put fruit and water for washing, and we burn incense.
I decided to take some of the objects we use in Puja into school in order to make a shrine for the assembly. Sue and Chris helped. I also had some slides (my interest in photography came in very useful) of my family performing Puja so we used them as well.
The Assembly went well. Sue and Chris remembered what I had told them about the objects. You could still smell the incense at lunchtime when we went in for school dinners! I suppose prayer and worship are as important as eating and drinking for me.

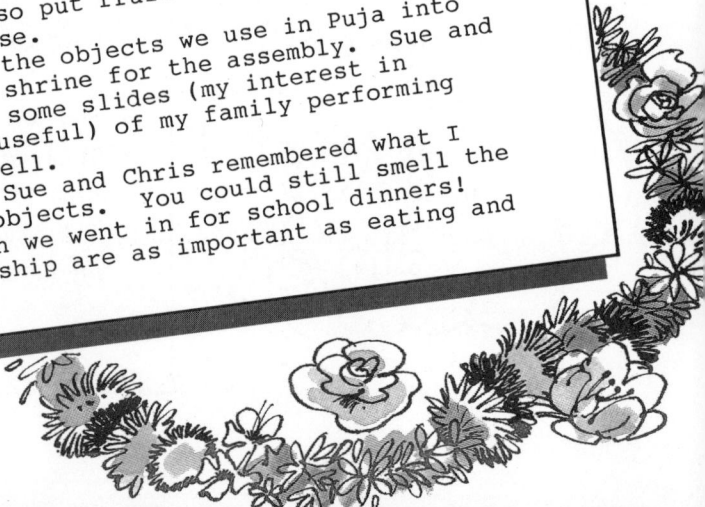

Task 13

1. Re-read the story and make a list of the special words Rakesh uses in his description of Hindu worship. What do these words mean?
2. What happens at Puja? Write down the actions Rakesh's family perform. What do they mean?
3. What signs and symbols are used in Hindu worship? Write them down and say what they express.

Extension work

A

Collect or *find* pictures which show the special objects which are used in Hindu worship. *Make* a model of a shrine and *label* the items.

B

If possible, *watch* a video about Hindu worship.

From what you have learned about communication, can you think why music and dancing are frequently used in Hindu ceremonies and festivals?

If you are Hindu or if there are Hindu members of your class you have a great resource, a great way for the class to find out more about Hindu worship.

Exploring Christian worship

A Folk Mass *Read Garry's story*

Hi! My name is Garry. I've only got a minute to communicate with you! You see this is the evening for my Folk Group practice - I play the flute and I belong to St Mary's Folk Group.

Every Sunday evening at 6pm in our church, we provide the music for Mass. Usually, I'm in Church by 5.30pm so that we can practise the music before most people arrive for Mass.

The Mass is also called the <u>Eucharist</u>.

We usually begin with a lively folk hymn and then, during the time when the community expresses sorrow for their sins we play some quiet music and sing 'Lord have mercy'.

I have to concentrate quite hard because after the first Scripture reading, we play and lead the congregation in singing the Psalm before the Gospel reading. We have to come in on time! When the Bread and Wine are brought up to the altar - it's time to play the Offertory hymn. After Communion, that is after we have gone forward to the altar and received the Body and

Blood of Jesus from the Priest or one of the men and women who help (they are called Extraordinary Ministers of the Eucharist), we play a hymn or a reflective piece of music.

After a time of silence, the Folk group leads the congregation in the final hymn, and all go home 'to love and serve the Lord', as the last blessing says.

I really enjoy being in the Folk Group and I enjoy Folk Masses. Many young people in our parish some along and join in. There's lots of joy around!

Task 14

Answer the following questions.

1. What is a Folk Group?
2. What kind of instruments provide folk music?
3. How would a Folk Mass differ from a more traditional Mass?
4. Why does Garry enjoy belonging to the Folk Group?

Extension work

A

Have you any favourite hymns?

Make a list of the top ten hymns of your class. If you go to church, *name the places* in the service when hymns are usually sung – (Garry mentions a few)!

Find out if your parents and older people like Folk Masses – Why? Why not? What are their favourite hymns?

B

Why is singing an important part of religious worship?

What kind of worship do young people like? What kind of worship do older people like?

ASSESS your work!

How did we do?

Tasks 13–14

1. *Describe three things in Rakesh's description of his family worship that particularly struck you.*
2. *Describe three things in Garry's description of the part he plays in his Folk Group that you particularly liked.*
3. *Did you learn anything new from Rakesh's and Garry's stories?*

Getting in touch with other people

Look back at the work you did in Tasks 1–7.

Remember what we felt communication was about or usually involved ...

sharing your thoughts and feelings/listening and responding to others/communicating and responding through words, with signs and symbols as well as other means of expression.

Task 15

Now, let's explore and describe how people communicate and respond to each other in the four contexts of life experience:

● **family community**

What is your experience of how people in families share their thoughts and feelings? How do they listen and respond to each other? How do members keep in touch with each other?
– through being together
– words
– actions
– signs and symbols

● **local community**

What is your experience of how people in your friendship groups
– in your school
– in your leisure activities
– in your local communities
communicate and respond to each other – by sharing time together through words, actions, signs and symbols?

● **the many faiths and cultures – the plural dimension**

What is your experience of how people communicate and respond to each other
– within their cultural or faith groups
– between the various groups
– is there an inter-faith group?

● **and the global or world-wide community of peoples**

What is your experience of how people communicate and respond to each other
– in other parts of the world
– as a world-wide community, e.g. Sports Aid '88?

Extension work: group activity

A and **B**

In groups, *choose* one of the sections above. *Share* with each other your experience. On a large sheet, *write* down your findings.

Display your sheet so that all the class can share your discussion.

Invite other groups to add to your group's sheet if they have new suggestions to make.

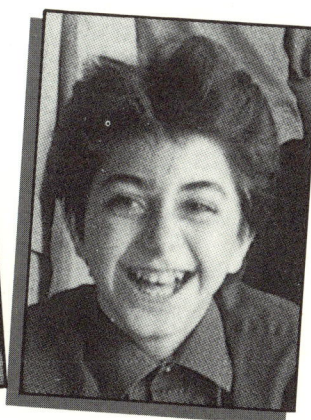

In touch with the natural world

Read Claire's story

I work in Chester in a famous department store. I won't advertise! A few weeks ago, I took my summer holidays and with a couple of friends toured the north of Scotland - It was beautiful. A real change from the city. You may have heard about the disease which is killing off seals - well we had first-hand experience of that. In a cove near Mallaig (you can find it on a map of Northern Scotland) we saw a number of seals which were suffering from the disease. There were volunteers from the local RSPCA working there.
When I returned it really struck me how beautiful nature is and how sad it is to think that pollution may be the cause of the death of a whole seal population. I've joined a local conservation group ... want to buy a flag...?! I've decided to do something about it!

Now ... choose and investigate one aspect of the world of nature in your locality or in the wider world where you think people could be more in touch with, or more aware of the dangers to, animals or plant life or important resources.

What actions are called for which might change the situation or prevent the situation becoming worse?

Some examples – a local river or common/the rain forests/the ozone layer and the use of aerosols/seals/whales/disposal of toxic wastes ...

Extension work

A GROUP WORK
Make a display which shows your concerns about the environment.

B
Write a letter to your local paper, or write an article for your school magazine to communicate your ideas about one aspect of the natural world in your locality that you think people should respond to: it could be something good, or it could be something that might be improved.

In touch with yourself

Billy's Diary

October 16th

What a day that was! Helen (who is 10) wouldn't get up for school, as usual, so breakfast was a real bundle of laughs, I don't think. Mum got really bad-tempered, Dad hid himself in the paper and the weatherman on the radio said rain and more rain. School was awful – when I eventually got there (the 76 never comes on time). Mr Burgess said I looked like a drowned rat and marked me late for school for the second time this week. Tom was off and he's got my chemistry book so Miss Patel chewed me up. P. E. went really well – I got really involved in gymnastics and felt relaxed and then there was Maths which is bad enough but Sir said the trip to Holland is full so it's not even worth saving up for it. When I got home I did baked beans on toast for everyone because Mum's on the late shift but Helen wouldn't wash up so there was another argument this time with Dad. I'm really glad I've got my own room to come to now. I really enjoy having some time away from all the hassle listening to cassettes and having a think about things, and writing my diary. I have a sign on my door – it says Ssshhh! Genius at work!

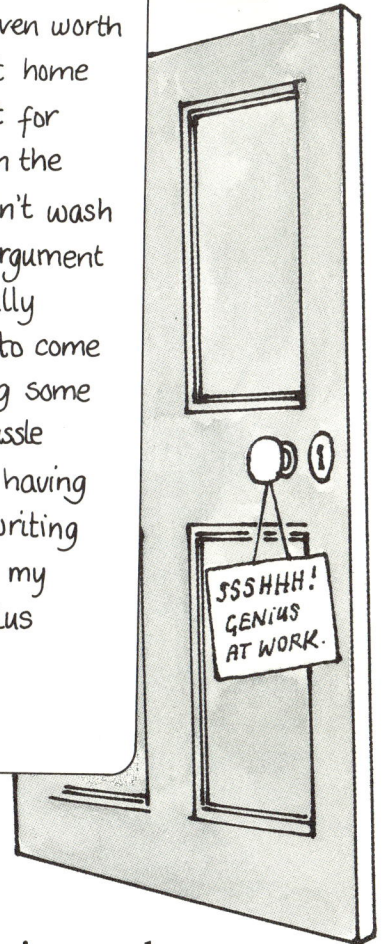

SSSHHH! GENIUS AT WORK.

Task 17

Read the extract from Billy's diary and try to answer the questions, by yourself or with a partner.

1. Why do people keep diaries? What do they write down in them? Who reads them? What goes into a diary?

2. What do you think about diaries? Do you keep one? If so, say why you do.

3. Why does Billy enjoy having a room of his own to go to? Where do you go when you want peace and quiet . . . at home/in school/in the neighbourhood?

4. Your experience – is it difficult at times to spend some time quietly at home or in school? Why, what factors make it easy or difficult? What about your neighbourhood?

5. If you want to get to know other people, the best thing to do is to spend some time with them. If you want to get to know yourself better, the 'inside story' on you, how would you go about it?

Extension work

A

When you get home this evening, try *writing* a diary, and *talk* about the experience in your next lesson.

B

Read some extracts from a famous diary: e.g. Anne Frank; Samuel Pepys; Adrian Mole.

Look again at question 1 in Task 17, and try to *answer* for the person whose diary you have read.

Silence and stillness

Task 18

Find a quiet place somewhere, sit quietly and spend five minutes in complete silence, with your eyes closed.

Afterwards compare your experience of silence with your friends.

What did you hear? How did you feel?

Repeat the experience but concentrate a little more on yourself:

- sit upright but not stiffly
- relax your muscles, be aware of the tension going out of them
- breathe easily, slowly and deeply
- try to be very, very still

Afterwards, talk with your friends and your teacher about this experience.

Extension work

A

Is there much silence around you? Do you welcome silence or not? Try to *explain* your answer to this question. *Make a poster* of all the words you can think of which describe feelings associated with silence.

B

Do a class survey on the number of people who have personal stereos or stereos/radios in their bedrooms. *Find out* how many hours are spent listening to music and how often people just sit in silence.
or
Find out why most supermarkets or superstores now have music playing all the time.

Would piped music in school help you to work better?
or
Write about yourself. Do you need to be silent at least occasionally? *Why* is it important to you? *What* does it do for you?

Exploring mystery

Are you good at solving word puzzles/number puzzles/crosswords?

Let's think about puzzles and mysteries

Puzzles

Can you do a Rubic cube or the Rubic Clock?

Can you finish playing solitaire and get the last peg in the centre hole?

Puzzles may be very difficult to do but they can be solved! There is a solution that can be found. Many problems in mathematics or science are like that too.

Many of life's more difficult questions do not seem to have easy answers or solutions. They are questions that have been asked since the beginning of time . . .

Why is there pain and suffering? How did the world begin?

Is there a God, a heaven? Does life have a meaning?

Many people feel that they can begin to answer some of these questions because of what they believe – but few people claim to know all there is to know about these **MYSTERIES**.

WHEN'S TEA?

I'M A KNOW ALL

Task 19 GROUP WORK

Some groups should work on the task in the left-hand column, and the rest on the right-hand column.

Make a list of ways of finishing this statement:

What really mystifies me about life is . . .	**What really amazes me is . . .**
Bring to the class some pictures which communicate or express what mystifies you.	*Bring to the class some objects which express or communicate the wonder of life to you . . .*
Talk about why they do so.	*Talk about why they do so.*

Extension work

A

Make a list and then a *collage* of all the things which amaze or mystify you personally.

B

Work out why three of the amazing things or events *are* amazing. Try to *communicate* your findings to the rest of the class.

I AM AMAZED!

More about mystery

mystery (Greek work *mustèrion*, Latin word *mysterium*)
something hidden which has been revealed,
something unapproachable which invites investigation,
something unknowable which offers true understanding.

Many people who have wondered at life and thought about the mystery of it all, have found and expressed their response to mystery in religious belief.

For example: pondering the mystery of how the world came to exist, many people have concluded that there must be a Creator responsible for its existence. Christians believe that in Jesus they come to know the God who created the world, and whom they call 'Father'.

Task 20

Reflect on the statements given below:

❝What really mystifies me about life is the fact that everything that lives must die.❞

❝What amazes me is that I have met people who go on loving people who treat them really badly.❞

❝I read about a Catholic priest who went to the gas chamber in place of another man. He did this because the other man had a family. This really amazes me.❞

❝I'm always amazed when the sun rises every day.❞

From what you have learned about Christianity, how do you think a Christian might respond to these statements?

Extension work

A

In your own words, *describe* what 'mystery' is.

B

Write an essay with the title: 'The mystery of human existence'.
or
Use some art form – painting, movement, drama, music, to express your understanding of 'The mystery of human existence'.

ASSESS your work!

How did we do?

Tasks 15–20

1. *Did you share your experience of how people communicate in the contexts of family, community, plural and global society?*
2. *What is the 'natural' world?*
3. *Did you try keeping a diary?*
4. *What are the main things which mystified people in your class? What amazed them?*

Your own experience of prayer and worship

Task 21 — GROUP WORK

Reflect on what you have learned about communication. Perhaps this is a time to look over some of the work you have done in this module.

Reflect on prayer and worship as ways of communicating. What do you think people are doing when they pray and when they worship? Perhaps you can talk about your own experience (if you wish to) or describe what you have seen people doing which you consider to be part of prayer and worship.

Someone in the group should act as the 'reporter' of the discussion. The report should include the main ideas that are discussed, and some of the examples or stories that are told in the group.

Extension work

A

Listen to the groups report back to the whole class.

Then, *write* two short paragraphs beginning

"When people pray, they . . . "

"When people worship, they . . . "

B

Explore the meaning of **'worship'**: look it up in the dictionary. Can you find the Old English word it comes from?

Reflect on the things you spend time with: are these activities 'worth it'?

Exploring prayer

Read Jane's story

I am really busy most of the day. I have to get up quite early to get to work in time. I like the journey on the bus in the mornings because there are lots of different people all making for school or work or the shops. It keeps me in touch with ordinary everyday life. I work in a children's hospital as a nurse. I love my work and I love the children. Some of them are very ill and it makes me sad, but often they are full of courage despite the pain they have and that makes me want to make them as comfortable as possible. I love to see their faces light up in a smile and hear them

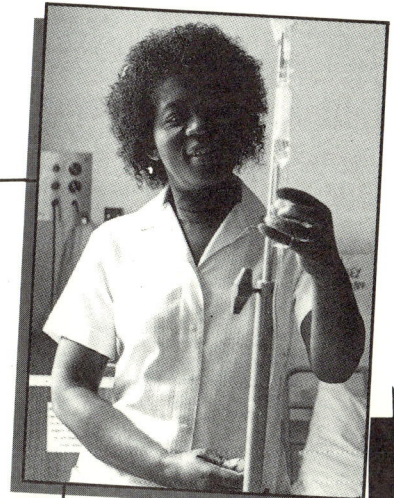

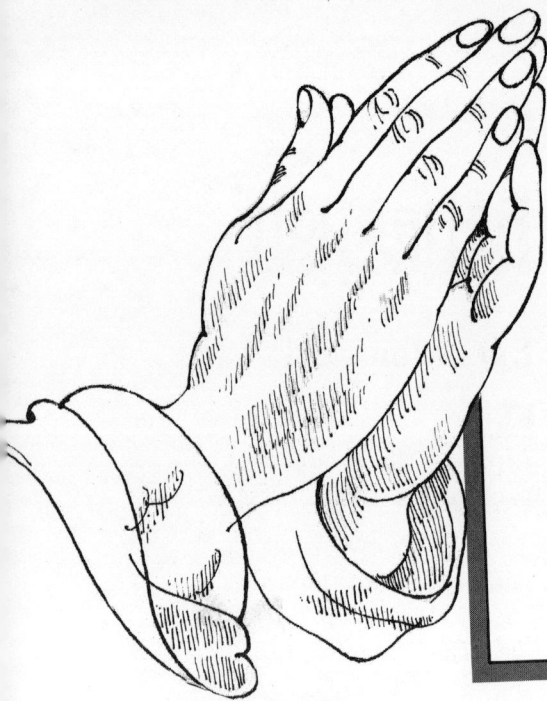

laughing. It's great to see them get really well, well enough to go home. Sometimes I'm very tired by the time I get home, but I need time to reflect on the day and offer it to God. It reminds me that everything I do is a kind of prayer and that God is there with me and the children I look after.

This quiet time gives me time to thank God for the chance to work with so many gifted and wonderful people who try to bring healing to children. When I go to chapel on a Sunday – I'm a Methodist – I join in the praying and the singing with the others and this is another way of showing how important God is in my life. It's another way of keeping in touch with God, of communicating with God and letting God communicate with me.

Occasionally I see some of the children I have nursed and that makes me feel great to see them well..... I sing louder!

Task 22

Answer the questions below in your file/workbook.

1. What kind of experiences in Jane's work as a nurse make her reflect?
2. Have you ever had any experiences like that? Write about one of them.
3. Jane says that her whole life is a prayer. What do you think she means?
4. In what different ways does Jane feel she communicates with God?

Extension work

A

Find out about Methodist worship.

Why is singing an important part of worship in some traditions? *Why* especially in Methodism?

B

Investigate a religious community where monks or nuns spend their lives in personal and community prayer.

If possible *invite a speaker* to your class who is a member of a religious community. What is life like for people like this?

Jesus taught his friends to pray

Task 23

Read the following.

Jesus' life and his ministry were very demanding, and he often went off by himself to pray. The people he called to follow him and to carry on his work asked him to teach them to pray.

The prayer he taught them became a very important part of every Christian's prayer, and of Christian worship as well: it is known as the Lord's Prayer, and all Christians are united in praying it.

Another name for the Lord's Prayer is the 'Our Father'.

Here is what Jesus prayed:

Our Father, who art in heaven,
hallowed be Thy name, Thy kingdom come,
Thy will be done on earth as it is in heaven.
Give us this day our daily bread,
and forgive us our trespasses
as we forgive those who trespass against us.
And lead us not into temptation,
but deliver us from evil. Amen.

The above is a 'traditional' version of the Lord's Prayer.
Let's think what these words mean.

Jesus taught his followers to

- *call God Father.* He used the Jewish word 'Abba', which means 'Daddy'. Some people today like to think of the idea of 'father and mother' here: God is the one who can be completely trusted.

- *call God holy*: for Jews, the name of God is so holy it must never be spoken.

- *pray for God's kingdom* – about which he preached all through his ministry – to come in our world; *and that all should do the will of God.*

Below is a 'modern language' version. (from the Alternative Service Book 1980)

Our Father in heaven,
hallowed be your name,
your kingdom come,
your will be done,
on earth as it is in heaven.
Give us today our daily bread.
Forgive us our sins
as we forgive those who sin against us.
Lead us not into temptation
but deliver us from evil.
For the kingdom, the power
and the glory are yours
now and for ever. Amen.

- *pray for human needs.* Just for today, not to stockpile for the future.

- *pray for forgiveness*, and learn how to forgive others.

- *pray to be protected* from the temptations and powers of evil.

Now, write in your own words a prayer like The Lord's Prayer.

Extension work

A and **B**

Mime the Our Father, using gestures only, no words.

Here are some other examples of Christian prayer. Read them slowly and then write in your own words what they say about God and Jesus.

The Creed:
the statement of what Christians believe about God

1. *This is from the Creed*

66 We believe in one God, the Father, the Almighty, maker of heaven and earth, of all that is, seen and unseen. 99

2. *This is from one of the Eucharistic Prayers (no. 4):*

66 Father, you so loved the world that in the fullness of time you sent your only Son to be our Saviour . . . To the poor he proclaimed the good news of salvation, to prisoners, freedom and to those in sorrow, joy. 99

Eucharistic Prayer:
the great prayer of thanksgiving at the centre of the Mass or Holy Communion service.

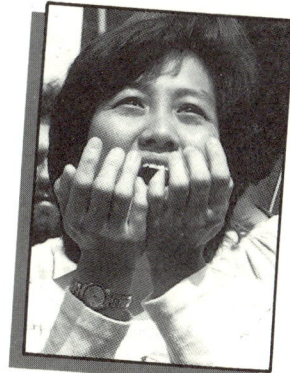

Ways of praying

There are many different ways of praying. People who pray use different ways at different times.

If you want to pray, then here are some ideas which will help you to do so.
If you do not want to pray, then just read the rest of this task quietly, because some of your class may be praying and may want some peace and quiet.

Task 24

This task will examine silence as one way of praying.

Silence

You live in a very noisy world – school noises can be deafening.

At home you may have the television on all the time, or you may be tuned into your personal hi-fi. This exercise is about being quiet and still.

1. Sit comfortably in your chair . . . try having a straight back and do not cross your legs.

2. Put your hands on your lap.

3. Now, begin to listen to all the noises around you/or in the street or in the corridor . . .
   Listen, and then try to forget them.

4. Be aware of your body sitting on the chair . . .

5. Now be aware of your breathing . . . breathe slowly . . .
   You may be a bit excited or feel like laughing . . . just relax and make your breathing steady.

6. Now . . . think about these words, very slowly . . .
   'I thank you Lord for my life.'

7. Say the words very slowly . . .
   every time you breathe out say 'I thank you Lord'
   as you breathe in, say 'for my life'.

After a few minutes slowly stop your prayer. Perhaps you will want to thank God for this quiet time.

Silence is part of prayer . . . if you want to keep a friendship up with your friends there are times when you have to be silent with each other.

Reflection

Extension work

A and B

Have you ever prayed or felt like praying?

When? What did you do?
If so . . . did you say prayers that you had learned or did you use your own words?

Is praying worthwhile?

Have you ever seen or heard·someone pray?
Why do you think they were doing that?

If not . . . Do you think that they were doing something worthwhile?
What do you feel about it?

ASSESS your work!

How did we do?

Tasks 21–24

1. *What have you learned about prayer from these modules?*

2. *Do you agree that worship is like communication? In what ways?*

3. *Can you say in your own words what the Our Father is? What does it teach Christians to pray for?*

Review of the module

And now
- look over the work you have done in this module. Describe which part of this module you enjoyed most. Say why.

- Look through your workbook, or the project work you have done and decide which work in your opinion is the best. Say why.

Before you read on . . .
- Write down all the things which you have learned during this half-term's work.

- What did you find most difficult? Say why.

- Which part of the module did you find uninteresting?

. . . just a minute . . .
Suggest ways of making this module more interesting.

We are the Champions!

Managing your own learning

Were you
1. Usually on time for class/usually late for class?
2. Hardworking . . . most of the time/some of the time/not very often?
3. Able to work by yourself sometimes?
4. Able to work with others in a group?

Did you
5. Find the work very easy or very difficult?
6. Work when the teacher was busy with other people or only when the teacher was with you?
7. Cooperate with the teacher?
8. Did you follow up any of the work you did at home by reading or finding out more about any of the topics you have covered?
9. Did you do any extension/project work?

Do you
10. Find it easy to tell the teacher of any problems you had?
11. Prefer to work by yourself or with others?

Now, share what you have done with your class teacher.

Congratulations! **You have completed Communication Level One.**

This module of work is called

Celebration

It is all about how people celebrate special occasions and experiences in life.

It is also about the important part that celebrations and festivals play in religion.

Here are some of the things you will be doing in this module on Celebration:

- **exploring** special occasions
- **describing** celebrations in your family and local community and in the global community
- **identifying** different elements in celebration
- **exploring** the idea of life as a journey
- **noticing** how religion celebrates special times in life
- **finding out** about the sacred thread ceremony in Hinduism and Sikh Amrit
- **investigating** Christian confirmation
- **thinking about** Christian sacraments
- **finding out** about the Christian calendar
- **reviewing** and **assessing** your work

Special moments

You have been around for quite a long time now. If you are just eleven years old then you have lived through more than **four thousand days** or about a **hundred thousand hours**.

Just think of all the things that have happened in that time.

Task 1

Copy the chart below into your workbook or file, and then fill it in. (Ask your teacher for help if you are not clear about it.)

A Moment You Remember	Describe the Experience	How Did You Feel?	What Did You Do?
A Very Happy Moment			
A Sad Time			
A Funny Incident			
A Fright			
A Big Mistake!			
A Success			

Extension work

A

How many more examples of each kind of experience can you remember?

B

Can you *add* to this list of experiences? If so, *describe* what happened, say how you felt and what you did, in the same way as above.

Celebrations

WHO IS YOUR FAVOURITE...

A celebrity is a person who is famous enough to be widely known and recognised.

This is a clue to what **celebration** means. **Celebration is a way of marking or recognising the importance of a special occasion or event or person.** Some celebrations are about very great occasions, and some are about what may not be earth-shattering but are still rather special to us personally.

Extension work

A

Write a short poem celebrating your favourite celebrity.

B

Which celebration have you enjoyed most of all? *Why* do you think that was?

Task 2

Think back over all the celebrations you have been involved in, from small-scale

'You've done well today – have an extra Smartie.'

to large-scale

'WE ARE THE CHAMPIONS!'

Make a list in two columns

The Reason for Celebrating	How it was Celebrated
1. e.g. last day of term	extra chips! mufti day etc.
2.	
3.	
4.	
5.	
6.	
7.	
8.	
9.	

Celebration in the community you belong to

A community celebration on a special day (or for a longer period) is sometimes called a **festival.**

Task 3

Working in groups, prepare a collage of celebrations in your community. Explain your work to the rest of the class, then display it.

Plan this task
You will need pictures from magazines, photographs, decorations, etc.
You may include captions, labels, and explanations.

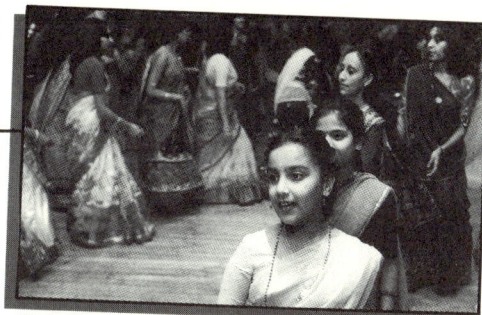

Celebrating in the local community

Celebrating in your town or district

Celebrating at home and in the family

Extension work

A

Interview an older person in your community. *Find out* about any celebrations which he/she remembers: what was special about it?

B

Prepare a short news bulletin on 'Celebrations in the news this week'.

Celebration in school

Celebration is part of life. You will spend over 11 years at school!

Task 4

Can you remember any school celebrations which you have been involved in? Write about the reasons for the celebrations and the way they were celebrated.

What kind of things to do with school should be celebrated? And how should they be celebrated?

Here are some occasions from the school year which you can think about . . .

1B's HARD WORK

A NEW MEMBER OF CLASS

A SUNNY DAY

YOUR FAVOURITE LUNCH IS ON TODAY'S MENU

Extension work

A

What groups are there in your school that may have something to celebrate during this school year?

B

Write a short paragraph about any *memories* which your school celebrates: e.g. remembering a *person*; remembering an *event*.

Reflect and discuss.

Are there any achievements and successes that your school community could celebrate more than it does. Which? and how?

School Assemblies

Task 5

On your own

Reflect

Then copy out and fill in the bubbles

I remember one Assembly when.....

I think Assemblies should......

At Assembly I usually........

A funny thing happened at an Assembly when.....

I think.....

Sometimes I feel......

Assemblies are.........

I would make Assembly more interesting by...........

At an Assembly in junior school I........

Some people I would like to invite to Assembly are......

Extension work

A

Describe a time when there was a feeling of celebration at an Assembly in your school. Do you think you could be more involved in planning, or participate more in Assembly? *How?*

B

List some features of school life that might be better reflected or celebrated at Assembly: e.g. school music-groups, choir, pupil artwork, community service, drama. *Which* members of staff might you put your suggestion to?

GROUP WORK

Share what you have written with the other members of your group.

Discuss what you think Assemblies are for.

Consider if any of the words below are useful for your discussion:

express	successes	worship	participate	reflect
performance	experiences	discover	gathering	information
presentation	talking-point	community	surprise	communication

33

Exploring celebrations

A local newspaper in Manchester invited its readers to describe how they celebrated New Year. Here is what one young reader sent in.

Task 6

Read this article

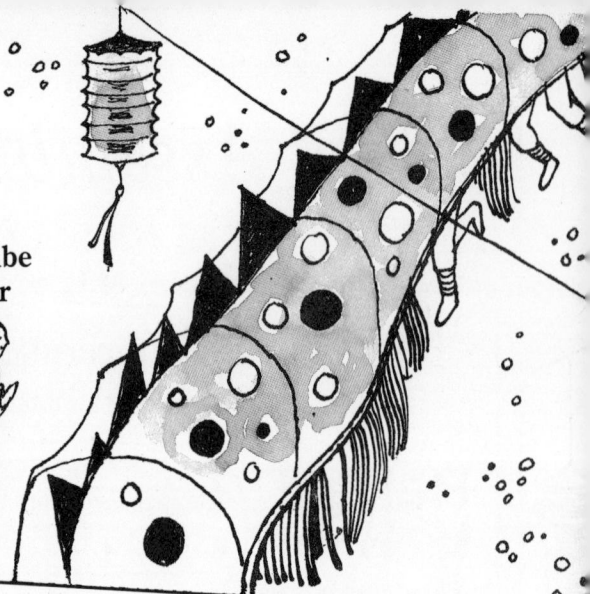

NEW YEAR CHINESE STYLE

by Wing Yin Ho aged 12

Most people in Manchester celebrated New Year last week, on January 1st, but for the Chinese community in Manchester the new year starts a little later, in fact this year it's at the end of January.

That's because our calendar is lunar (that means, it's based on the phases of the moon) and New Year is the first day of the first month of the calendar, usually about the end of January or the beginning of February. It's great for me, because I enjoy all the excitement of Christmas and New Year with my friends at school (especially the way that the streets are decorated in town, and the huge Santa and his reindeer on top of the Town Hall) and then we have our own special Chinese celebrations with all the lights and decorations.

It's important to start getting ready for the New Year at least a week before. I don't always like housework but it's exciting when all the family are helping to make our house just right for New Year. The kitchen has to be really clean because our tradition says that the kitchen god makes a report on the home before the festival starts. On the evening before New Year, we welcome the gods back by lighting firecrackers and burning incense.

It's a smashing time in my family. My brother who works in London always comes home for New Year, and we visit all our friends and relations, and of course we remember people who are no longer with us.

As it's the start of a new year, we wear new clothes and we try to make it up with anyone we have had a quarrel with. Last year my brother even gave me back my Michael Jackson LP that he had borrowed months before.

Of course, the parties go on for days and we eat a special kind of dumplings called Jiaozi, some with coins hidden in them. My uncle always gives me 'lucky money' inside a red envelope and my sister and I shake the coins from the money tree. It's a way of looking forward to good fortune in the year ahead. Our house is always filled with flowers and decorations and, of course, presents. We dance and sing and have processions in the street, and my brother is one of the dancers in the monster dragon. The next Year of the Dragon is 1996. Everything finishes with a special celebration called the Lantern Festival, where the bright lights remind us that spring is coming after the dark cold nights of winter.

Now

Look back over the article you have just read.

The list below mentions various things that might be found in a celebration.

Can you find an example of each of these in Wing Yin Ho's story?

Copy the table into your workbook, and write alongside each entry the part of her story that you think fits it best.

Celebration	*Chinese New Year*
Community which is celebrating	
Reason for celebrating	
Preparations	
Ceremony (special act)	
Words and gestures	
Food, drink	
Decorations	
Special clothes	
Music, dancing	
Gifts	
Symbols	
Feelings	
Deeper meaning and values	

Extension work

A

Think of a birthday party you have been to, your own or a friend's. How many of the features in the list apply to the birthday celebration?

. . . a few, most of them, or all of them?

Make a new chart, starting . . .

Celebration	*Birthday*
etc.	

B

A **ceremony** is a special part of a celebration where set words and actions are used to point to the deeper meaning or purpose of the celebration.

for example:
the lighting of a torch, the parade of athletes and flags and inspiring words at the opening ceremony of the Olympics.

Describe a ceremony you have attended or taken part in.

Was there an element of 'doing things *properly*', or in the way they have 'always been done'?

Can you think of other ceremonies where there are fairly definite rules to be followed? If so, *make a list* of them and *compare* your list with your partner's.

ASSESS your work!

How did we do?

Tasks 1–6 were about your experience of celebrations.

1. *Did you explore special moments in your experience?*
2. *Did you examine some reasons why people celebrate?*
3. *Did you work in a group to plan some work on how your community celebrates?*
4. *Can you recall the main elements in a Chinese New Year celebration?*
5. *What is a ceremony?*
6. *What celebrations and ceremonies does your school especially value?*
7. *What progress do you think you have made in this module so far?*
8. *Which piece of work or activity are you most proud of?*
9. *How was it recognised or celebrated?*

Celebrating all over the world

It's unlikely that anybody in the class has not had something to celebrate, or not enjoyed a celebration at some time or other. **That's because celebrating is an experience shared by human beings all over the world – it is natural for people to want to celebrate. In fact some celebrations actually remind us that we belong to a world of people who share very similar hopes and ideas about what is important in life.**

Task 7

Brainstorm, as a class, celebrations around the world that show how wide-spread is the experience of celebration. Suggest all the celebrations that young people of your age in other countries may take part in.

> **for example:** harvest festivals; Remembrance Sunday; Mardi Gras; special saints days; Divali . . .

By yourself, or with a partner, choose one of these celebrations and collect information about it.

Use the checklist in Task 6, of aspects of celebration, as a guide for your work.

(You may be able to do this from your own memory, or from TV programmes or films you have seen, or books you have read.)

Share your work with the rest of the class.

Extension work

A

Make a list of all the countries whose celebrations have been described in the work done on Task 7. *Find out* where they are on the globe.

Do you think there are people anywhere in the world who have never ever had the experience of celebrating?

B

Can you think of any recent celebrations which have helped to bring home to people that they are united with people of other countries and nationalities in celebrating a particular cause, event, or person?

What could you add to these suggestions?

Have you been involved in celebrating in this way? What did you feel like at the time? What did you learn from it?

Religious Celebrations

A great many of the customs, traditions, and festivals that people celebrate have a religious purpose or religious aspects. Just as celebration is a world-wide human experience, so too celebration forms part of what most religious believers do.

Task 8 — Research

There may be a variety of cultures and religious backgrounds represented in your class, your school and your local community.

Find out: What celebration may be particularly special to the members of these cultural groups? How do they celebrate as families? How do they celebrate as a community?

Remember: People themselves are a valuable source for your learning.

Think about and decide ⟹ *Which of the celebrations you have found out about are religious celebrations? Say why you think so.*

Extension work

A
Find out which religious celebrations are taking place in your local community during the time you are studying this module.

B
Make a calendar of customs, festivals and celebrations taking place around the world during the time you are studying this module. *Mark* with an asterisk those that have a religious connection or purpose.

Your experience of a religious celebration

Task 9

Think of a religious celebration that you have been involved in or attended, or that you have heard about from your friends. This might include a festival which is celebrated nationally in your country (e.g. Christmas in Britain).

Look again at the chart in Task 6, and use it to reflect on your experience of the religious celebration or festival you have experienced.

Extension work

A
Describe how you felt during the celebration or festival last time it was held.

B
Reflect: how important do you think celebrations like this are in your community?

Celebrating life as a journey

Have you ever thought of your life as a journey? Many people have looked at life this way, and have thought of all the experiences that people have on journeys as being a good way to reflect on and celebrate life.

Task 10

Describe (briefly) a famous journey made by someone recently or in history, e.g. Ian Botham crossing the Alps; Hannibal crossing the Alps; someone sailing/rowing/flying the Atlantic or around the world.

Do this now.

Next,

Can you find in your description (or did you mention) any of the following ideas:

> the purpose of the journey
> preparation for the journey
> setting out
> companions on the journey
> people met with on the way
> difficulties encountered
> getting lost, finding the way again
> signposts, milestones, resting-places
> reaching the end

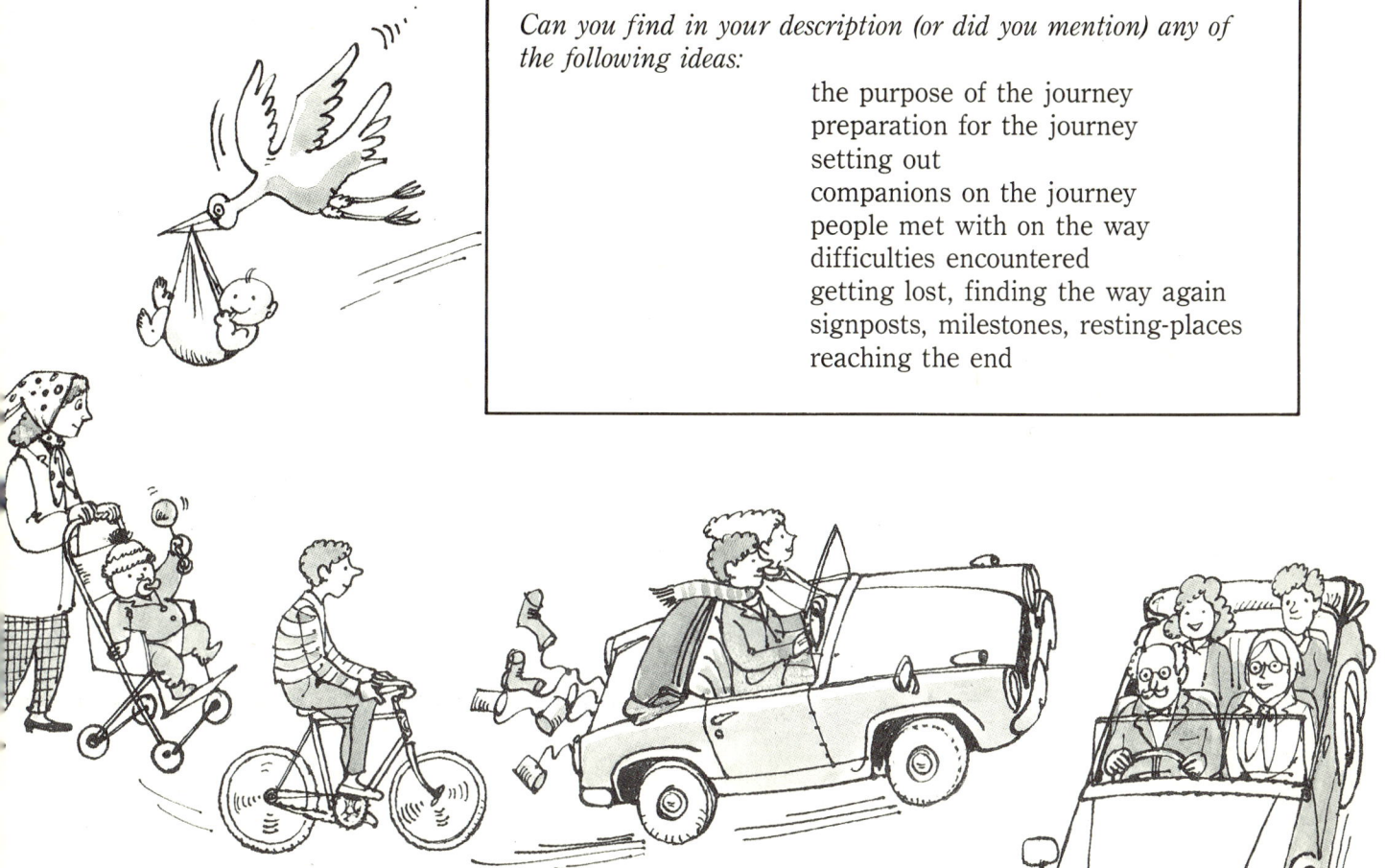

Extension work

A

Write about or *tell* your partner about any journey you have made, mentioning some of the happenings listed above.

B

Why do you think people have often used the idea of a journey as an image or picture of what human life is like?

Task 11

With your partner, map out the most important experiences that will mark out the passage through life for baby Ruth. She has had the very first experience – the whole process of birth. You decide what the rest will be. You may think of them as stepping stones, milestones, turning points, crossroads, etc. You might find the list in Task 10 helpful.

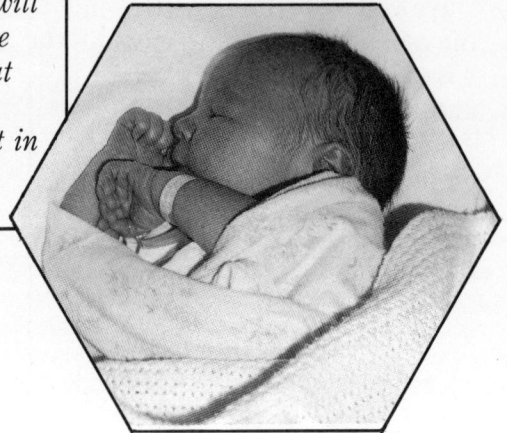

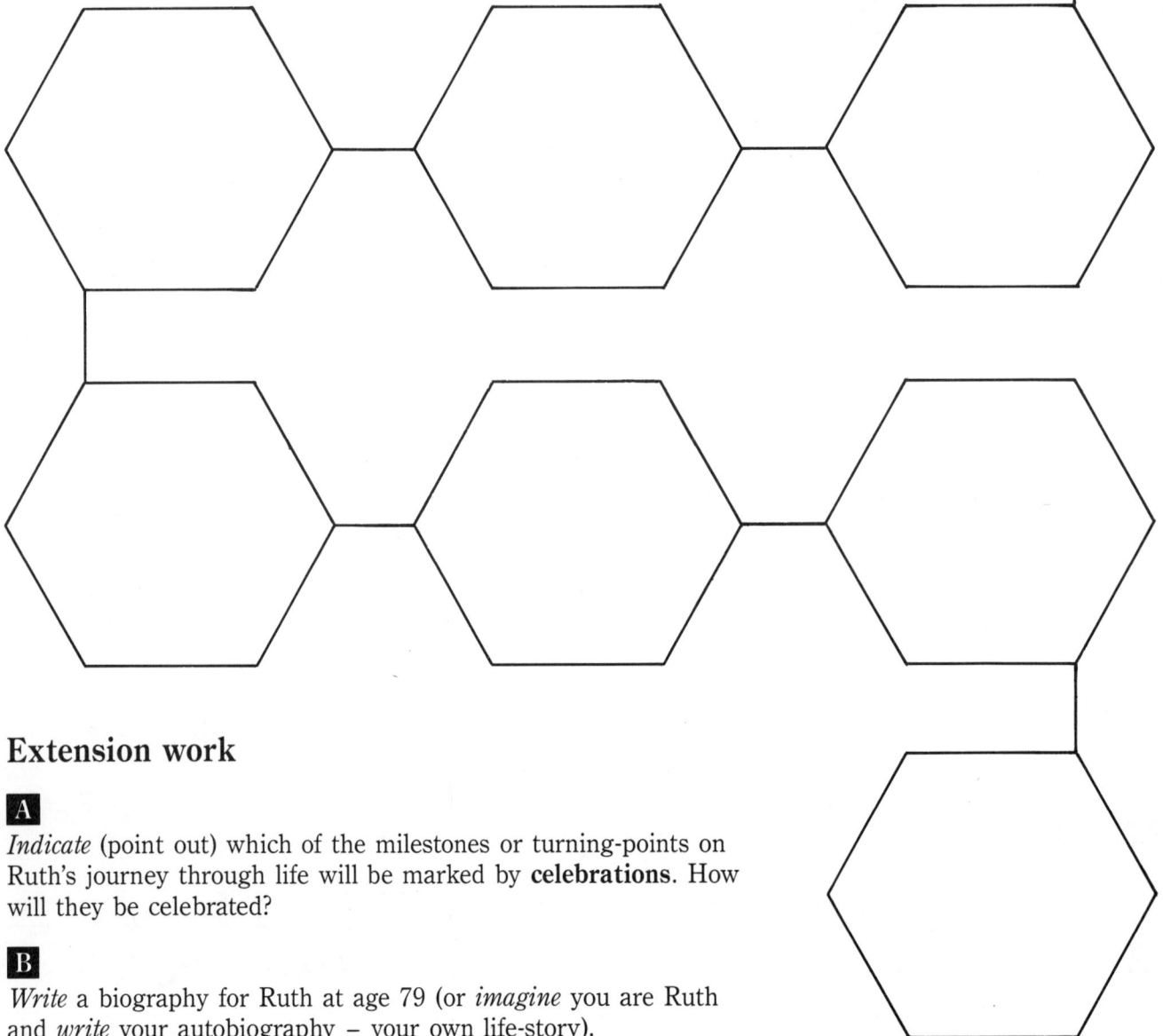

Extension work

A

Indicate (point out) which of the milestones or turning-points on Ruth's journey through life will be marked by **celebrations**. How will they be celebrated?

B

Write a biography for Ruth at age 79 (or *imagine* you are Ruth and *write* your autobiography – your own life-story).

40

Celebrations in religions

All religious traditions celebrate a person's passage through life, especially the main stages.

In their celebrations, religions include all the elements that you described in Task 6, but they go beyond them.

Religious celebrations

- explore and express the mystery of life
- reflect deeply held beliefs and values
- usually include prayer and worship

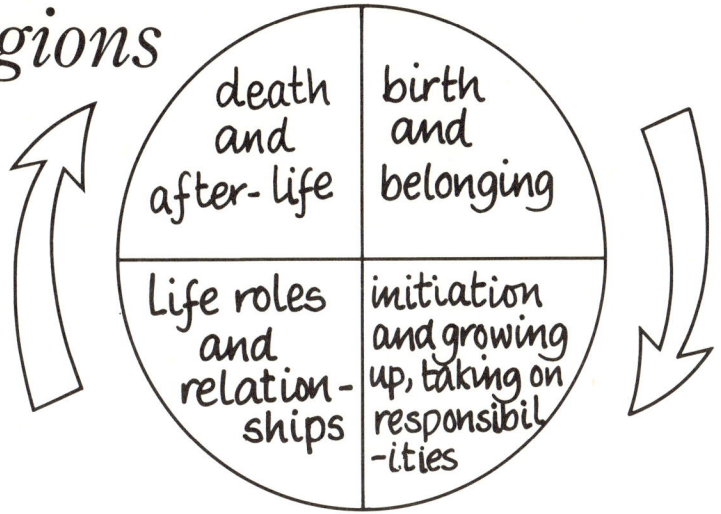

death and after-life *birth and belonging* *Life roles and relation-ships* *initiation and growing up, taking on responsibil-ities*

Task 12

In the first module of Level One on Community you explored the first ceremonies of birth and belonging in Christianity and in Hinduism. What do you remember about these?

Briefly review your learning about baptism and naming ceremonies.

Extension work

A

Answer these questions

1. Why are names given such importance at birth ceremonies? How did you get your name? Does it have a special meaning?
2. Why do some families give the same name to a child as its parent or grandparent had?
3. *Make a list* of the main duties of a parent towards a son or daughter. Did you find these duties were emphasized (given a special part) in the baptism and naming ceremonies?

B

When children are young their parents make lots of decisions for them. Do you think that parents should decide to bring up their children in a particular faith?

Give your reasons.

Tasks 7–12

In Tasks 7–12 you explored how celebrations happen wherever there are people.

You also looked at religious celebrations, and celebrating life's journey.

1. *Recall one celebration from another country or culture which you explored. Write a short paragraph about it.*
2. *What religious celebrations have been experienced by your class group?*
3. *Why are there religious celebrations? You may want to read Task 8 again.*
4. *In what ways is life like a 'journey'?*
5. *Which part of the journey have you reached?*
6. *Remember baby Ruth? What do you remember about her?*
7. *How do religious traditions celebrate the main stages in a person's life from birth to death?*

Extension work

Did you do any?

Have you any work to complete before you move onto the next part of this module . . . ?

Now, move on.

Celebrating growing up in Hinduism

In the next part of this module you will be exploring how Hindu young men celebrate another special time, when they take on the responsibilities of being a Hindu. The ceremony is called the Sacred Thread ceremony.

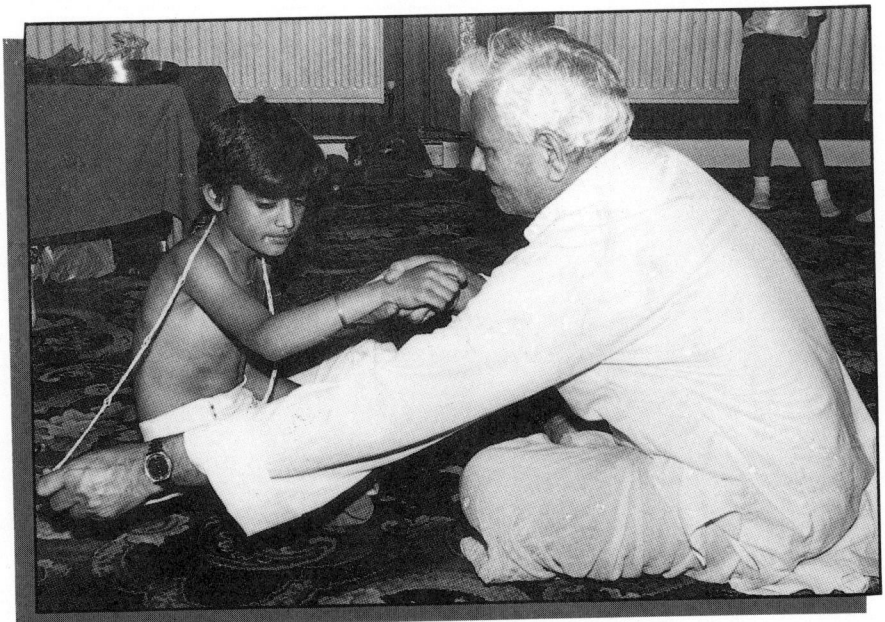

The picture shows Damodar receiving the Sacred Thread.

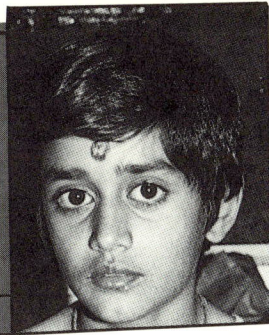

My name is Damodar. I am 12, I live in Southall in London, and I am Hindu. Just recently I received the Sacred Thread, in a ceremony which marks the fact that I am now taking on the duties of being a Hindu. The proper name for this ceremony is the Upanayana, and what happens is that a thread which is made up of two links, each with three cotton threads made up from three strands, is given to the young man. He wears it over his left shoulder and tied below the waist on the right side.

When I was much younger, I asked my father what the thread was for. He told me it is a symbol of the three main gods of Hinduism. I expect you may know that they are called Brahma, Vishnu, and Shiva – the Creator, the Preserver and the Destroyer. My dad said that when you have the thread on, it helps you to remember that God is all around you, and that your faith is true and of real value. The strands also help to remind you to keep a tight rein on your body, your mind and your speech.

Before you receive the Sacred Thread you have to do a period of strict preparation. I remember watching Daley Thompson getting ready for the Olympics and thinking that in a way I was getting ready for my big day in the same way.

It's a very special day of course and all your family and friends are there – a real celebration. When the instructor gives you the Thread he says,

'This sacred thread is pure and will lead you to know God.'

But it's not all over then – that's only the beginning. You have to go on to do some study of the sacred books of the Hindu community and learn the prayers or mantras which are used in Hindu worship.

Not everyone receives the sacred thread these days – I suppose it's because in Hinduism we feel we have to adapt to new ways of living and some of our customs have to change. Often young men receive the thread just before marriage, to show that they are committed to a Hindu way of life.

Now, answer these questions

Knowledge

1. Describe the Sacred Thread and how it is made up.
2. Where does Damodar wear the thread?
3. Name the gods which the strands represent.
4. What has to be done before the ceremony?
5. What had to be done after the ceremony?

Understanding

1. Why do Hindus receive the Sacred Thread?
2. What does the thread symbolise?
3. Why do some Hindus not receive the Sacred Thread nowadays?

Evaluation

1. Do you feel it is right that some big occasions demand a period of strict preparation? Have you ever experienced anything like that?
2. Can you imagine what it feels like to be involved in this ceremony?

Extension work

A

The Sacred Thread ceremony applies to young men only. In the community you live in, are the ceremonies or symbols of being a young adult the same or different for girls and boys?

B

Are there any differences in the responsibilities that young men and women have in your community?

Do you think young people get responsiblities too early or too late where you live?

The Sikh celebration of commitment

Saminder Singh and Davindra Kaur are brother and sister – and they are twins. They are eighteen years old and in the Sixth form of their school in Bristol.

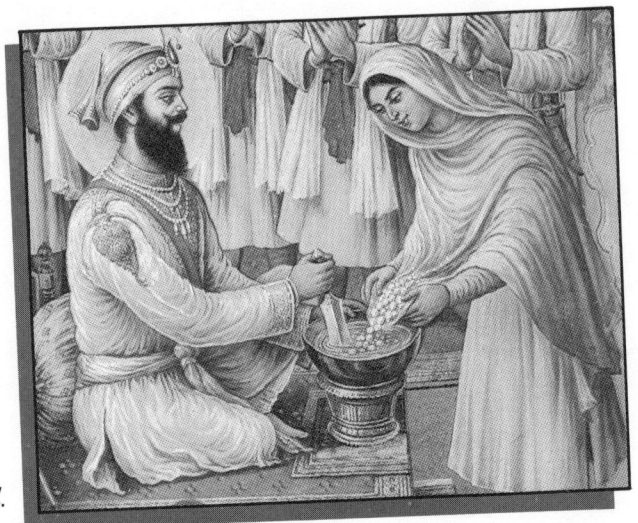

An illustration from a Vasakhi greetings card.

44

They recently had this article published in the school magazine.

ALL ABOUT AMRIT

Lots of people in school have asked us about what it is like to be a Sikh so when the Editor asked us to write an article for the magazine we decided to tell you about a special ceremony that Sikhs have, which is called Amrit. You have to be at least sixteen to be baptised as a Sikh, and there have to be six Sikhs and a Guru Granth Sahib present. What happens is, one of the community explains the responsibilities of being a Sikh

to love God
to read and study the Adi Granth
to serve humanity

and during the prayers that follow the Amrit (a mixture of water and sugar) is prepared. Five Sikhs, who represent the Khalsa or brotherhood founded by Guru Gobind Singh, kneel on one knee and stir the bowl with short swords. The nectar is then sprinkled on your eyes and hair and hands five times and you drink the rest of the Amrit. Then everybody shares karah prasad. From that day you must obey all the vows of Sikhism.

Task 14

Read the story of Saminder Singh and Davindra Kaur.

Do you remember what the Guru Granth Sahib is? Explain this to your partner.

What happens during the ceremony of Amrit?

What responsibilities did the twins take on?

Why do you think it is necessary to be at least 16 before a person can take part in this ceremony?

Extension work

A

Describe the responsibilities gradually taken on by people in your community as they grow to adulthood.

B

Consider whether you think responsibilities and commitments are a burden or an opportunity.

The Christian celebration of confirmation

Do you remember?

In the module on Community, you saw that Christians become members of the Church community through the celebration of baptism. Do you remember Maria Gomes' story?

Baptism can take place when a person is an adult, but it is more common when they are very young.

For Christians who have been baptised as young children, at the request of their families, there comes a time when they are invited to complete their 'initiation' into the membership of the church, and celebrate their 'confirmation' as church members, as committed Christians. This is done at different ages in different dioceses, quite often with teenagers.

In fact, for most Christians there are two celebrations of belonging and commitment after being baptised – Confirmation and Holy Communion or the Eucharist.

Initiation means 'becoming a member of'

In this module you will be looking at the *celebration of confirmation* in the Roman Catholic church.

" You have already been baptised into Christ and now you will receive the power of his Spirit and the sign of the cross on your forehead. "

" Let us pray to our Father that he will pour out the Holy Spirit to strengthen his sons and daughters with his gifts and anoint them to be more like Christ the Son of God. "

" On the day of Pentecost, the apostles received the Holy Spirit as the Lord had promised . . . "

" You must be witnesses to Christ's suffering, death and resurrection; your way of life should at all times reflect the goodness of Christ . . . Be active members of the Church . . . give your lives completely in the service of all, as did Christ. "

" The Holy Spirit fills our hearts with the love of God, brings us together in one faith . . . and works within us to make the Church one and holy. "

Dear Aunty Georgia,

Tues 4th Apr.

Thank you for the confirmation present and card you sent me. It was a lovely day even if I was a bit nervous at first. The church was full with all our families and friends and the Bishop had a big cloak on and a tall hat and a shepherd's crook (Dad said it's called a crozier.) He (not my Dad - The Bishop!) explained what being a Christian means. He reminded us that when we were baptised our parents and godparents had made promises for us, and he asked us to make those promises now for ourselves. Then we stood up and said yes, we believed in God the Father, and Jesus his Son, and the Holy Spirit. Each of us stood in front of the bishop: Aunt Jenny was my sponsor, and she put her hand on my shoulder. The Bishop dipped his thumb into a little pot of oil - called chrism. (Our teacher said this is the oil that is used to anoint kings and queens.) and made the sign of the cross on my forehead. Then he said the words of confirmation: 'Karen, be sealed with the Gift of the Holy Spirit' and I replied 'Amen.' He gave me the same greeting Jesus gave to his friends: 'Peace be with you' and I answered 'And also with you.' It was all very solemn. When I went back to my seat, Mum and Dad hugged me. Then we went to Communion.

Love Karen.

sponsor
a person who supports another person.

Task 15

Read Karen's letter.

Why do you think her sponsor put her hand on Karen's shoulder? Discuss this with your partner.

What did the bishop's words to her mean? (You might be helped in answering this if you read some of the sentences in the boxes, from the words the bishop spoke to the people being confirmed.)

Extension work

A

Why are Christians confirmed?

B

If you have been confirmed, *describe* your own confirmation celebration.

ASSESS
your work!

How
did we
do?

Tasks 13—15

1. *What do you remember about the Sacred Thread ceremony? What does it mean for young Hindu men?*
2. *What is Amrit? Which religious group celebrates it? Why?*
3. *Can you describe part of the confirmation ceremony? Can you explain what it means for young Christians?*
4. *Did you do any extension work? Which did you enjoy best?*

Celebrating the sacraments in Roman Catholicism

Catholics believe that Jesus Christ is present in the community which is called the Church. They celebrate the presence of Jesus in their lives in the seven sacraments. In the celebration of the sacraments Catholics come together to hear the word of God in Scripture and to express – through the use of symbols such as water, oil, bread and wine – their belief that Jesus is with them and gives them strength to live in his way.

In this module, in Task 11, you will have considered Ruth and the stages she might pass through on her journey through life. People celebrate special moments in their lives: the birth of a baby, birthdays, getting married. In the sacraments, Catholics celebrate Jesus' presence at special moments, and are strengthened in their journey through life.

Let's explore this a little further. In other modules of *Weaving the Web* you will look at some sacraments in more detail.

Task 16

Look up the following references in the New Testament, and work out how they relate to the sacrament in the photograph.

Remember – the name refers to the title of the book, the first number refers to the chapter of the book, the other numbers indicate the verses.

You may have studied signs and symbols in the module on Community in Task 14. Can you remember?

Baptism	Mark 1: 9–11 Matthew 18: 3 Acts 16: 25–34.	
Confirmation	Luke 4: 18–19 Acts 2: 1–4 Acts 8: 14–17	
Eucharist	Mark 6: 30–44 John 6: 34–40 Acts 2: 42.	
Reconciliation	Mark 2: 16–17 John 5: 21–22 Matthew 11: 28–30	
Sacrament of the Sick	Matthew 8: 14–17 Mark 1: 40–45 James 5: 14–15.	
Marriage	Mark 10: 6–9 1 Corinthians 13: 4–7	
Sacrament of Orders	Mark 3: 13–19 Mark 10: 41–45 Acts 6: 1–7.	

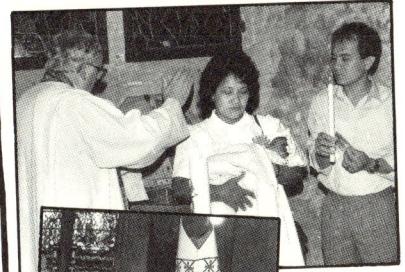

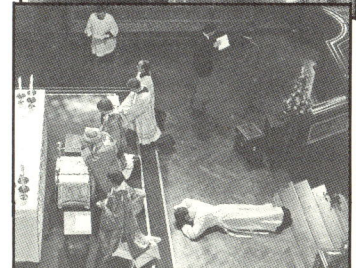

Extension work

A

In the module on Community you thought about symbols. Can you think of a symbol or symbolic action connected with each of the seven sacraments?

B

Can you *describe* in a few words what each symbol means for those who are celebrating the sacrament? Could you *explain* it to your partner or others in the class?

A major Christian festival
The Feast of Pentecost

Every year, normally in May, Christians celebrate the Feast of Pentecost.

This is how Simon, a first year student in Norwich, wrote up his project book on Pentecost:

I read the account of what happened at Pentecost in the Acts of the Apostles, chapter 2, verses 1-13, and I thought I'd try to write it down in my own words. The account in the Bible is in St Luke's words - St Luke wrote the Acts of the Apostles.

Before I begin my story, I'll fill in some of the background details: For 40 days after Jesus' resurrection (that is, after he was raised from the dead) he appeared to many of his followers. He told them to stay in Jerusalem, not to go away. They had many things to ask him: and he promised to send the Holy Spirit to them, to strengthen them in the work they had to do to teach others about the Kingdom of God. They saw Jesus ascend to heaven (Luke tells about this in Acts 1:10) and they went back then from Mount Olivet to Jerusalem.

I found out why it is called Pentecost. Pentecost is a Jewish feast which celebrates the time after the first harvest of cereal crops. The celebration takes place fifty days after. Pentecost comes from the Greek word for 50. This is how to write Pentecost in Greek.

πεντηκοστη   50 days after the beginning of the barley harvest and the end of the wheat harvest.

<u>Pentecoste</u>

As the first Christians were Jews, and as Pentecoste happened 50 days after Easter Sunday, they used the same word for their great day. (I love details like this).

This is my story of Pentecost.

When Pentecost day had come, all the special friends of Jesus, including his Mother, were gathered in an upstairs room with the door locked. Suddenly, there was a very loud sound like a tornado or a very strong wind howling.

...The sound filled the whole house where they were. As if that were not enough, there appeared something that was like flames of fire and each flame rested on one of the apostles and on Mary the Mother of Jesus. It was really frightening. They were all filled with the Holy Spirit, just as Jesus had promised. And the Spirit enabled them to speak in other languages so everyone could understand them.

I think that the power of the Holy Spirit on them was really amazing. It transformed them from very frightened people into courageous ones who were able to come out of the locked room and go into the streets and preach about Jesus.

Task 17

Read this story in Acts 2: 2–4.

Role play this scene.

Discuss with your partner the symbols used in this story. What do you think they mean? Make a collage to show the power of wind and fire.

What happened to the friends of Jesus. Describe them before and after the event described.

Look at your collage: how do these symbols express the change that took place in the disciples.

Extension work

A

Can you see any connection between the first Pentecost experience and Karen's confirmation in Task 15?

B

What similarities and *differences*, if any, do you see between the Christian Church today and the early Christian community?

Exploring Christian festivals

Task 18

Copy this table into your workbook.

Look up the references given in the left-hand column.

In the space next to each reference, write the event in Jesus' life described in the biblical reference.

The next column gives you the name of the festival which celebrates the event.

In the last column, put the approximate time of year when this takes place.

Reference	Event	Festival	Time of Year
Luke 1: 26		Annunciation	
Luke 1: 5–2:5		Advent	
Luke 2: 6–20		Christmas Day	
Matt. 2: 2–12		Epiphany	
		Ash Wednesday	
		Lent	
Luke 19: 28–40		Palm Sunday	
Luke 22: 7–19		Maundy Thursday	
Matt. 27: 27–54		Good Friday	
Mark 16: 1–8		Easter Sunday	
Acts 1: 6–11		Ascension Day	
Acts 2: 1–4		Pentecost	
		Trinity Sunday	
		Halloween and All Saints	
		All Souls	

Extension work

A

With your teacher, *discuss* how *Ash Wednesday* and *Lent* came to be important times in the *Christian calendar*. (Look for evidence of Jesus fasting and preparing for the events of Holy Week.)

B

Find out what Christian beliefs are celebrated in the last three festivals on the list.

Task 19

Choose any Christian feast or celebration.

Find out about it.

Is there anything about the feast in the Bible?

Which scripture readings are used to celebrate this feast? (You can find this out from the Lectionary.)

The Lectionary is the book which contains all the readings from the Bible that are used for Christian celebrations in church.

Extension work

A

Do you have a favourite feast or celebration? If so, *say* why you like it best.

B

Compare the Christian feast you have chosen with a celebration from another religion. What do they have in common? What is different about them? (You may find the checklist in Task 6 useful here.)

ASSESS your work!

How did we do?

Tasks 16–19

1. *Can you name the seven sacraments which are celebrated in the Roman Catholic church?*
2. *Do you know what each celebrates?*
3. *Can you describe in your own words the story of what happened at Pentecost?*
4. *Name some Christian festivals. What does each one celebrate?*

Review of the module

What do you think is the most important thing you have learned? What was the hardest part to understand in the module? Which part of it did you enjoy working on most?

How could this module have been improved? Can you think of anything which would have made it more interesting and enjoyable?

In general, do you think your work on *Celebration* Level Two is better than your earlier work? If so, in what way?

We are the Champions!

Managing your own learning

Were you

1. Usually on time for class/usually late for class?
2. Hardworking . . . most of the time/some of the time/not very often?
3. Able to work by yourself sometimes?
4. Able to work with others in a group?

Did you

5. Find the work very easy or very difficult?
6. Work when the teacher was busy with other people or only when the teacher was with you?
7. Cooperate with the teacher?
8. Did you follow up any of the work you did at home by reading or finding out more about any of the topics you have covered?
9. Did you do any extension/project work?

Do you

10. Find it easy to tell the teacher of any problems you had?
11. Prefer to work by yourself or with others?

Now, share what you have done with your class teacher.

Congratulations!

**You have completed this Level Two module.
You should feel free to celebrate your achievements.**

This module of work is called

Values

It is all about what people value most in their lives, and especially about the values which arise out of religious beliefs.

There may be more to do in this module than you have time for. Possibly there will be extra activities which you and your teacher would like to include.

You may also need to think ahead and plan for some of the activities in the module – for example inviting a speaker (Task 9) or arranging to do a survey (Task 18) – your teacher will help you with this.

Here are some of the activities you may be engaged in:

- **exploring** your personal values and attitudes

- **describing** some of the choices and decisions you commonly make

- **identifying** some values in the community you belong to, at home and at school

- **carrying out** a project on values in your local community

- **thinking about** the values expressed in the media

- **finding out** about some values for young people in India

- **discovering** the values which Hindus live by, especially those expressed in a Hindu marriage service

- **exploring** values in Christianity

- **assessing** your own progress in this work

- **reviewing** the work of the module

- **managing** your own learning

Enjoy your learning

Just before you start, can you identify the four strands of experience in *Weaving the Web*?

The symbols below may help you to remember . . .

1.

2.

3.

4.

1. ....

2. ....

3. ....

4. ....

Can you explain to your partner what each of the strands is?

Now look at the top of this page, at the list of activities in this module. Can you identify which strand of the R.E. programme is being dealt with in each activity? Which symbol would go next to each of the activities in the list?

You will notice that each of the strands is woven into this module on values.

Now get weaving!

Exploring personal values

Task 1

Read this story . . .

Jimmy McGrain's Story

It was nearly four o'clock, and Jimmy started to put his books away, ready for a quick start when the bell went. He had a special reason for wanting to get home early.

'You can start putting your things away now — it's nearly time for the bell,' said Miss O'Keefe, 'Except you, Jimmy. I want a word with you.'

The rest of the class left, and Jimmy shifted restlessly from one foot to the other while the teacher tidied away the rulers and scissors.

'I told your mum yesterday that you needed extra help with your reading and spelling, Jimmy, so I thought we might spend half an hour on it now.'

'I can't, Miss. Honestly!'

'But Jimmy, it's very important for you to improve your reading and . . .'

Jimmy ran out of the room.

Next morning, Miss O'Keefe was waiting, and she didn't look very amused. Jimmy steeled himself.

'It's your attitude that's the problem, Jimmy. Your reading and spelling are very weak; so is your number work. You don't seem to have your mind on your class work, and you don't really seem to care. Then, when I give up my time to help you, you run off. That's not a very responsible thing to do, is it?'

'You see Miss, I've got a chicken in the back yard at home. She hasn't been very well, Miss, so I wanted to go to the library and find out what to do about it.'

'I see, Jimmy. Well, what did you find?'

'There's a lot on chickens in the encyclopedia, Miss. Did you know that they've been reared for over 4000 years? They come from the wild red jungle fowl of ancient India. Anyway, it says that this species, *Gallus gallus*, gets dysentery if it's not fed the right kind of food. It needs a special kind of grain. So, I wrote down the name and went to the Vet. He told me that was the right diagnosis and sent me to a pet shop that had the grain. I worked out I could afford it if they'd let me pay in two instalments. Then I dashed home and fed my chicken. Do you know, Miss, she looked better this morning!'

'I think you'd better bring your chicken into school, Jimmy, and tell the class all about it. You're quite an expert!'

Dictionary work

Look up the word **Value** and write down what it means

Explain what a **Value** is to your partner

56

GROUP WORK

In your group, discuss the following questions about the story:

1. What was most important or worthwhile to Jimmy?
2. How do you know this – what evidence is there in the story?
3. Why was the teacher surprised?
4. Have you ever had an experience like Jimmy's?

Now consider what you feel to be some of the most important, worthwhile or valuable things in life.

Make sure that you contribute your own ideas in your group, but be careful also to listen to what the others say.

Working on your own, *Make two lists headed*

My values	Other values in my group

Extension work

A

Collect together all the values expressed by the members of your class. *Make a list* of them; then *pick out* the ten that are most important to you, and rank them from one to ten.

Compare your results with your partner.

B

Imagine that your country has been invaded by some rather unfriendly but very powerful enemy: life will be very different from now on.

What values would you want to defend with all your energy?

Write a brief letter to the invaders, outlining what you hope they will allow to continue.

Desert island

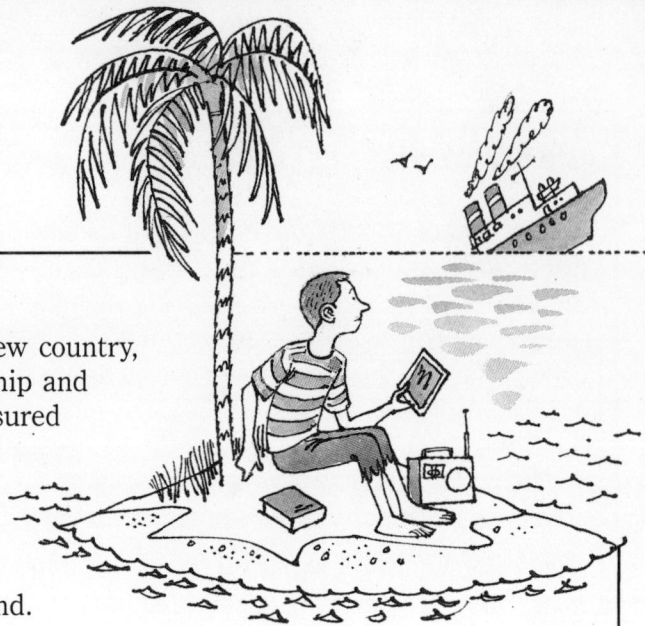

Task 2

You are travelling by sea to your new home in a new country, with all your possessions. A fire develops on the ship and you only have time to collect your three most treasured possessions before the ship goes down. They are
a photograph
a cassette player with music and batteries
a book

You cling to a plank and are washed up on an island.

By yourself: decide which photograph, music and book would be the ones you would take with you.

In a group: share this with the rest of the group and explain your choice.

Extension work

A

Write a couple of sentences about each of your choices.

B

Give reasons for your choice and compare with the rest of the group.

What sort of *values* underlie your choices?

Exploring attitudes

Task 3

This task concentrates on *positive* attitudes towards yourself and other people.

Copy this chart into your workbook or file and then fill it in. This work is about how you think, and might best be done on your own.

WHAT I VALUE MOST ABOUT			
Myself	*My Family*	*My Friends*	*My School*

Extension work

A

(If what you have written is very personal and private, you don't need to do this next exercise . . . but you may feel that you can share what you have written with your partner.)

Tell your partner what you have written, and then *listen* to what your partner has written.

Check that you have listened carefully, by trying to *describe* what your partner values.

Compare the two charts. *Find* similarities and differences.

B

If things were different, *what I would like to be able to value* about myself, my family, my friends, my school, would be . . .

Making decisions and choices

Task 4

Here are some people of different ages. They are all involved in making choices and decisions of various kinds.

GROUP WORK

For each person, try to work out in your group what sort of choices or decisions the person might have to make. Make a list of them all. Try to think of people you know who are at the same stage in life as the person you are considering. This may give you some ideas about the choices that people have to make.

Still in your group, pick out what you think is the most simple or least significant (important) choice or decision, and the most complicated, difficult or important decision or choice for each person. Does your group agree?

Your teacher will help you to arrange a way of sharing what you have discussed with the class.

With your partner make a list of the choices and decisions which you have made over the last twelve months. Are the choices and decisions any different from those of the people you were considering in the group work? How?

Dictionary work

Look up the word *priority*, and find out its meaning.

Express what it means in your own words.

Extension work

A

Make a diary for last weekend, mentioning any choices or decisions which you make. *Rank* the choices from *easy* or *trivial* up to *complicated* or *very important.*

B

Explain what is meant by, and give some examples of, the following kinds of choices or decisions:

a matter of taste
a question of personal interest
a matter of life or death
a random choice

a matter of principle
a question of convenience or expediency
a moral choice

Exploring priorities

Sometimes when you are faced with some decisions to make, or have to choose between two or more things to do, you have to work out if *one* of the possible choices is more important, or more urgent, or fits in better with what you really want to do. What you feel you should choose or you ought to do *now* is your *priority* at the moment.

Look at the cartoon: what do you think are priorities for the people in the cartoon?

Can you come to the concert Sue? I've got tickets

I'm not sure exam tomorrow / Anna, I've got an exam tomorrow and I need to revise.

Oh, go on! I need someone to go with – It's more fun.

I really don't think so, but I'll see what my mum thinks.

Mum, I need to revise but Anna's asked me to go with her to the concert. What should I do? / I think you'll have to decide that for yourself.

I'm late for work already and don't want the sack! ?

Priorities and values

Task 5

Work by yourself for a few minutes.

Make a list of the priorities for you and the people you live with. You don't have to mention anything which you feel is very personal or private, but you should be able to think of some priorities which you feel you can write down.

Draw a cartoon like the one on p. 59, showing one or more of the priorities for you in your situation.

Reflect on your work in this task. What values do you think are being expressed in your choice of priorities (what very important things lie behind your choices and decisions)?

Extension work

A

With your partner, *role play* the situations you have drawn or described in your work on the task.

B

Write a short scene involving some people of your age who are establishing some priorities for themselves.

ASSESS your work!

How did we do?

Tasks 1–5

Did you plan how you would approach the work in this module?

Have you prepared for later work that needs planning?

1. *Did you explore the story about Jimmy?*
   What is a value?
   Can you remember what you said were your values?
2. *What did you learn in the Desert Island exercise?*
3. *Did you complete the chart about attitudes to yourself, your family, school, etc.?*
   Did you attempt the extension work?
4. *Did you find it easy to think about the decisions that people make as they go through life?*
   What did you learn from what your class did in Task 4, making decisions and choices?
5. *Did you enjoy the cartooning, role play and script-writing in Task 5?*
   What is a priority?

Values in your school

For the work on this section, you need to arrange yourselves in your groups. **The task will involve**

Brainstorming
Giving feedback

Comparing
Video work (if your school has a video camera).

Task 6

Brainstorming

In your group, try to think of all the *values* which are promoted in your school. Here are some questions which may help you to think about this

- *what sort of things does your school community consider very important?*

- *what are the priorities of your school?*

- *is there anything that people in your class or your group are striving to do?*

- *what do other people connected with you (apart from pupils and teachers) value most in your school community?*

You should all record the ideas that come up, and then one person in the group should *collate* them – make one list representing the group's ideas.

Giving feedback:

Your teacher will help you to decide which is the best way to do this in your situation – perhaps displaying the lists, or by a quick report from each group.

If you are not one of the reporters, you should listen to the reports and look out for new ideas not mentioned in your group.

Comparing

With your partner, compare the list of values for your school with your experience of your primary school.

Are there any values which are the same?

Are there any values which are different, or missing?

Make a list of similarities and differences.

Video work

If your school has a video camera you can record the next activity as a brief advertisement.

Each individual in the class, working alone, writes down two or three ways of finishing off the sentence

'I would like to learn in a school where . . .'

Here is an example – it is what a first year pupil in a school actually wrote.

'I would like to learn in a school where you don't have to carry your bag and coat around with you all day.'

Find a way of including everybody in the presentation.

When you have made the video – discuss whether you think it would be of interest to anyone outside your own form group.

Extension work

A

Tape record a brief message for next year's first year, telling them about the *values* they may expect to find in their new school.

B

Write a letter to the Chief Education Officer or Director of Education telling him or her about the *values* at work in your school.

Values in the local community

Task 7

Plan:
How you will explore the values of your local community.

Decide
1. *Whether you will work* on your own, in pairs, *or* in a group.

Remember, this module is *not* encouraging you to go off on your own. If you decide to work on the project by yourself, you can still get the information you need while you are travelling to school or shopping with your family, or from your neighbours, or by writing letters, or in the local library.

2. *What questions will your project be trying to answer?*

Your teacher will help the class to decide this.

Here's an example:
What sort of things does the local community where I live seem to value?

- *the environment?*
- *the elderly, the disabled?*
- *young people?*
- *leisure and recreation?*
- *amenities?*
- *business?*
- *peace and quiet?*

How you will record *and* present *or* display *your work.*

Explore your local community's values

Present *or* display your findings

Extension work

A

Write a short letter or article for your local newspaper, or *make a tape* of your views, concerning the *values* you have found.

B

Find out what you can about the work of the Social Services.

Values in building up the community

Task 8 (You will need to have planned this particular task earlier on in your study of this module.)

Invite to your class someone who works in the community, trying to build it up – someone who you think values a particular aspect of local community life, e.g.

a social worker
a local councillor
a community health worker
a voluntary service person
a hospital visitor
a minister of religion etc.

Decide
Who will write or phone to invite the speaker?
Who will welcome and look after the speaker during their visit?
Who will thank the speaker on behalf of the class?
What do you want the speaker to talk about?

Extension work

A

Make a note of the questions and answers during the visit.

B

Prepare a display or assembly about the values expressed by your visitor.

A charter of values

Task 9

Draw up a charter (a list of priorities) of values for young people around the world. To help you to think about this, discuss what rights, freedoms and responsibilities young people have.

Your charter could then start with

We the young people of the world, value........

You could produce your charter rather like an illuminated manuscript, with a very decorative first letter and border.

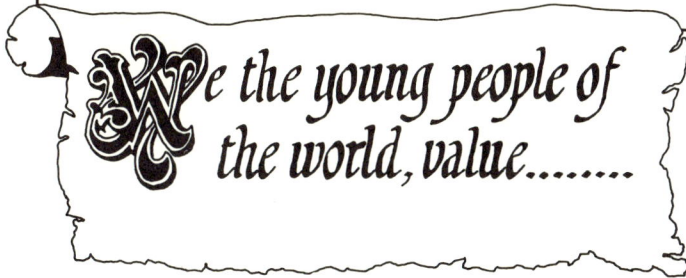

Extension work

A

Make your own personal charter of values.

B

Research the work of a United Nations agency concerned with young people.

Exploring global links

In this part of the module you will be exploring your links with people in communities around the world. You will be considering whether people in other countries are in any way important to you.

Task 10

Ask at home for an old shopping list that has been used for remembering what to buy at the supermarket or an itemised till receipt. Paste it into your workbook or file and then try to identify which country each item or its various ingredients come from. Draw a map of the world and connect up the place where you live with the places where your items of shopping come from. Make a larger chart and display all the class findings on the one map.

GROUP WORK

In small groups, discuss whether there are any conclusions to be drawn from what you have discovered.

Formulate (express as clearly and briefly as you can) your discoveries.

Extension work

A

Make a list of the tins and packets of food at home which come from other countries, and name the countries.

or

Ask permission at your local supermarket (choose a quiet time, and a note from your teacher may be helpful) to *trace where their products come from.* Are the lists different for different shops?

B

Sometimes people refuse to buy goods when they find they are from certain countries. Can you find examples of this?

Why, do you think, do people boycott certain products?

What do you think of that?

Now you can explore more widely

Task 11

In your group, write down all the objects you normally meet in the course of an average day or, at least, a selection of them.

So your list might start:

bed	toothbrush
mattress	trainers
pillow	uniform
alarm-clock	cereal
soap	sugar etc.

Then, work out from the label or from what you know, where the object or its raw materials originated (first came from).

e.g. trainers made in Taiwan

rubber from ....

plastic from ....

suede from ....

cotton laces from ....

I can look after myself.

Extension work

A

Reflection

Do you agree?
What do you think?

B

Imagine that you wake up one morning to find that everything in your home which originated from another country has been destroyed.

How do you manage?

ASSESS your work!

How did we do?

Tasks 7–11

1. *In Task 7 you were invited to explore the values in your school community. What was the result of this exploration?*

2. *In Tasks 7 and 8 you explored values in the local community.*
   Did you carry out a survey?
   How did people react to your questions?
   Did you find out what you needed to know?
   How did you tackle collating and displaying or presenting the results?

3. *Task 9 involved thinking about a charter for young people. What values did your charter promote? How many of these rights and freedoms do you have?*

4. *Tasks 10 and 11 invited you to explore the links you have with people in other parts of the world through everyday objects and foods. What did you learn from this activity? What do you think now – do people depend on each other more or less than you thought before this work?*

5. *How much extension work did you manage?*

Exploring media values – advertising

Task 12

Look at the advertisement.

What product is being advertised?
What is the setting or background being used to sell the product?
What image is given of people who use this product?
What values do you think are being expressed?

Now with your partner, make a collage of advertisements for various products or services.

Then make a chart, like the one below, in your workbook or file.

	Product	Setting	Image	Values
1.				
2.				
3.				
4.				
5.				

For each of the products in your collage, fill in the column in your chart.

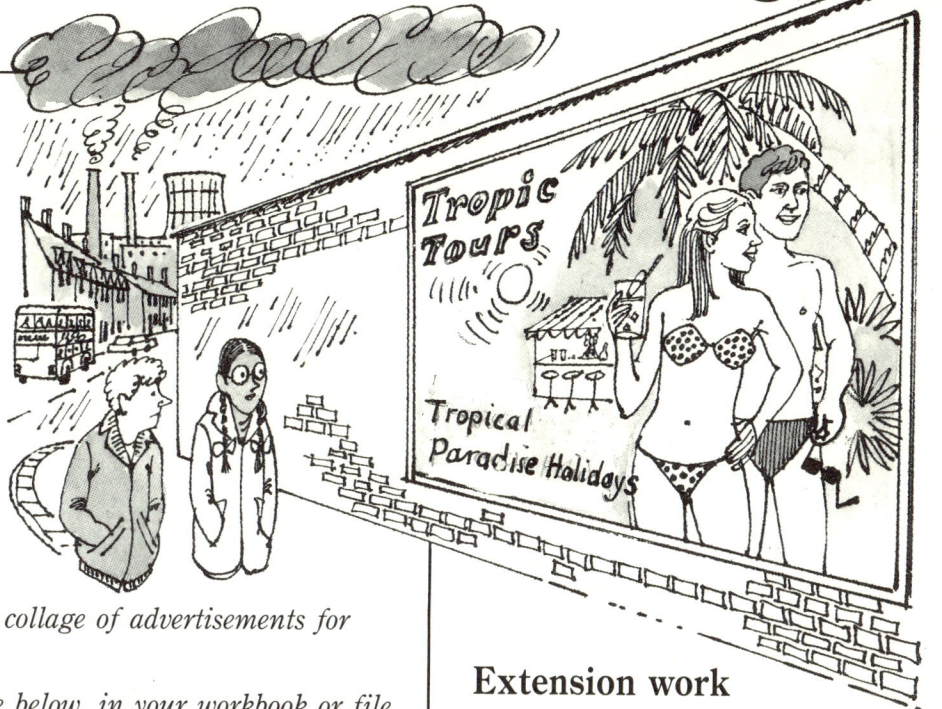

Extension work

A

What is each of your chosen advertisements *saying* about how you should live your life? Do you *agree* with what is being said?

B

In groups, *discuss* why advertisements are so successful in helping to sell products.

Media values – newspapers and TV

Task 13

For this task, everyone in the class will need one newspaper.

Each person should look through the paper very quickly – taking not more than a few minutes. Then swap with your partner and look through again.

Now, with your partner, discuss and decide what the editors and reporters of the newspapers think are important

Now, with your partner, discuss and decide what the editors and reporters of the newspapers think are important
worth knowing about
worth showing a picture of

What do they think their readers will enjoy?
be impressed by?
be concerned about?

Do any of the papers seem to value one kind of reader rather than another?

Report back to the class.

Extension work

A

Make a list of the ten most popular TV programmes in your region – or guess what they are.

Who or what do the programmes present as being
- successful?
- good to know?
- a nice neighbour?
- a typical young person?
- a good lifestyle to have?
- a modern way of thinking?
- an old-fashioned way of behaving?
- a very important issue to be concerned about?

Try and give an example for each.

Can you find any differences between children's TV programmes and those made for adults to watch?

B

What are the *values* expressed in a TV soap that you sometimes (or often) watch?

Media values – 'pop' culture

Task 14

GROUP WORK

Bring in some pictures of your favourite pop stars. In your group, discuss what you think is important or valuable in life for a pop star. What is a pop star saying about how life should be lived? In what ways is the pop star's life different from people of the same age in your community? In what ways is it the same? Is there anything you really admire about the star? Anything that bothers you?

Extension work

A

Lyrics. Write down some of the words of a pop song that you know and say what *values* are being expressed through the song – what does the song suggest is most important in life?

B

Reflect on the lifestyle of a pop star or group that you know something about. What aspects of that lifestyle either *appeal* to you or *put you off*? Give your reasons?

How did we do?

Tasks 12–14

1. *Task 12 was concerned with advertising.*
   What were the main values that came across in the material that you looked at?
   What do you think about the values expressed in advertising?

2. *How did you explore the values in the press and TV, in Task 13?*
   What did you find?

3. *What did you learn about values in the 'pop' world?*
   Did you find these values appealed to you and to your class?
   Why or why not?

4. *What have you learned from your work on the media?*

5. *Did you do any extension work for these tasks?*
   How did you do?

Family life and education
values in a Tibetan children's village in Northern India

Task 15

Read Pema's story.

Comprehension:
Why is education so highly valued in the S.O.S. villages?

Dharmsala
Amritsar
DELHI

Pema's Story

My name is Pema and I live in the Tibetan Children's village at Dharamsala in India. Ever since Tibet was invaded by China, there have been refugee and orphan children like me who have been cared for in the children's village.
It's a lovely place to grow up because the village makes sure that every child has a family to belong to and a really good school to go to. The older students when they leave here are able to get good jobs and become good parents of families themselves. Our teachers are all from Tibet and they help us to understand and love our land and it's people and customs. We say Buddhist prayers every day and we have had a visit from His Holiness the Dalai Lama, the spiritual leader of Tibet, who helped set up our school, and Mr Gemainer who started the idea of the S.O.S. Children's Villages, which are all over the world now.

Extension work

A

Make a list of the similarities and the differences between your experience of family life and school and Pema's.

Do you think family life and education are valued by the young people you know?

B

Research: Find out about an organisation in this country which is promoting literacy among adults who missed out on school as young children.

In the next two sections you will be exploring some values in Hinduism

Values of a Hindu family in Britain
a Hindu wedding ceremony and Hindu family life

One of the highest values for Hindus is that of family life. A family's home is the centre of Hindu life and worship, and Hindus believe that marriage is a lifelong commitment. Because marriage is so important, older members of the family play a part in choosing the marriage partner and arranging the wedding.

My wedding day
by Nandita Pradhan

There was so much excitement among my family and friends – I won't ever forget anything about the day I was married. I wore a beautiful red silk sari and many pieces of gold jewellery which I had been given. All the guests were given refreshments when they arrived, and the shrine where we were to be married (a sort of canopy), was beautifully decorated.

Then suddenly there was even more excitement because Virendra had arrived. You couldn't see Virendra's face because it was hidden behind a special covering – a reminder of when Hindu couples used to marry without having seen each other. Virendra was given yoghurt and honey, which is a symbol of welcome and of a happy life. We were ready for our wedding ceremony.

The priest lit the sacred fire and added incense and ghee (purified butter). Then part of my sari was tied to Virendra's scarf, and we walked around the fire together. Then I had to put my foot on a stone as a symbol of strong loyalty. Rice was poured into my hands, and from there into Virendra's hands, and he put the rice onto the fire. This is a symbol of growth and success. Then red dye was put on my hair and the priest told me I was now married.

At the end of the ceremony we took seven steps together around the fire.

The first step – for the sake of food
the second step – for strength
the third step – for wealth
the fourth step – for happiness
the fifth step – for children
the sixth step – for sustenance
the seventh step – for unity

Virendra took the veil from his face and we were showered with rose petals.

This is a picture of Krishna. Find a story about him.

Krishna

Extension work

A

Hindus worship the Lord Vishnu, in the form of Rama and of Krishna. Rama's story is told in a famous poem called Ramayana.

> Rama was a prince who was cheated and stopped from being king of a place called Ayodhoja. A demon king, Ravana, kidnapped Rama's wife, Sita, and carried her off to the island of Sri Lanka. Rama was helped by his brother Lakshmana, and the monkey god Hanuman and his army of monkeys, to rescue Sita from captivity. Then Rama regained power over his kingdom. For Hindus, Rama and Sita are the ideal husband and wife.

What qualities do you think an ideal husband or wife should have in order to have a happy marriage?

B

Find out about what happens at a Sikh wedding. What values are expressed in the ceremony? How do they compare with those expressed in a Hindu ceremony? *Write* a short fact-file on what you discover.

or

Talk to an elderly couple who have been married for a long time. *Ask* them what they value about their married life. *Record* their answers in writing or on tape. *Compare* what they say with the values expressed in the Hindu wedding ceremony. What are the similarities and differences?

Hindu values

For a Hindu, the main goal in life is to be set free from the endless cycle of birth and rebirth. This liberation (*moksha*) leads to being in union with Brahman, the supreme Spirit or Reality. The way to be set free is by doing the right actions, such as worship and helping other people.

For a Hindu there are three values which have to be blended together in life:
dharma – doing right, treating others fairly
artha – being prosperous and successful
karma – enjoying life

Task **17**

Role-play a situation where someone attaches importance to one of these values but forgets about the others. For example:

someone who is so eager to be wealthy and successful that he or she treats other people unfairly

or

someone who is so frightened about making even the tiniest, most trivial mistake, that he or she is unable really to enjoy life.

Analyse: what do you think? Is a balance of these values necessary for a good life?

Extension work

A

Make a brief *summary* of what Hindus value, from what you have learned so far.

B

Hindus believe that everybody shares in the divine; everybody has something of God in them.

What practical difference would it make in life to have this belief? What values would it involve?

ASSESS your work!

Tasks 15–17

1. *In your work for Task 15, did you reflect on the reasons why people value family life and education?*
   What do the S.O.S. Children's Villages do to promote these values?

2. *What have you learnt from your study of Hindu values in Tasks 16 and 17?*

Do you think these values are shared by other members of the community where you live?

3. *Did you enjoy the role-play about values? How did you rate your work?*

4. *Did you do any extra extension work?*

Values in Christianity

Task 18

What do Christians value?

This task involves you in doing an investigation into what a Christian group really values. You might choose members of

- a local church or parish
- L'Arche community
- the St Vincent de Paul Society
- the Young Christian Workers
. . . *or any group of your own choice.*

You will need to plan how you are going to do this in class:

1. Who are you going to ask?
2. Where are you going to ask them?
3. What questions are you going to ask them?
4. How are you going to collate (collect together) the replies or responses?
5. How are you going to present or display your findings?

Remember to keep your questions clear and simple. Now, carry out your investigation.

Extension work

A

Look through some Christian hymns and identify the values expressed. How do they compare with your survey?

B

Evaluate how some Christian communities (e.g. a parish community, a local church community, a Christian school community), live out the values expressed. What difficulties or problems are there in trying to do so?

Gospel values

The main source of Christian values is the person of Jesus Christ. His teachings and actions are presented in the Gospels of the New Testament. In this task, you will be exploring the values of Jesus expressed in what he said and did, as presented in the Gospels.

Task 19

For this task you will need a copy of the New Testament.

Look up each reference of the Gospels of Matthew, Mark, Luke and John. (The first number is the Chapter and the second number or numbers is the Verse: e.g. Matt. 5: 1–9 is Matthew's Gospel, Chapter 5, Verses 1–9.)

Decide what is important, or a value, for Jesus in the lines you have read.

Write down in your own words what this part of the Gospel tells us about the values of Jesus.

Matt. 17: 20

Matt. 16: 24–26

Matt. 15: 29–31

Luke 4: 1–4

Mark 3: 35

Mark 6: 31

Mark 10: 43–45

Mark 12: 28–34

Mark 2: 5

Matt. 18: 1–4

Mark 10: 17

Luke 21: 37–38

Luke 4: 43

John 4: 8–9

Luke 12: 29–31

Mark 14: 32

Luke 4: 16

Luke 12: 6–7

Luke 6: 32–37

Extension work

A

Look through the collection of sayings and incidents that you have found in the Gospels. *Choose* three of them which you feel give a picture of what Jesus valued most of all.

B

Compare what you discovered in your survey in Task 18 with the values you have found in the Gospels in Task 19.

Christian faith in action: A personal or group project

There are many thousands of people whom Christians respect for the way in which they lived out their Christian values. People of the past who are specially honoured in Christianity are sometimes given the title *Saint* (e.g. St Francis of Assisi, St Paul, St Elizabeth). There are also many Christians in the recent past who are not referred to as saints, but whose lives are an inspiration to others and a model of Christian faith in action.

Task 20

Choose an individual whose Christian faith and values are or were put into action in their lives, and prepare and present a small project on that person.

Some examples:
William Booth
Father Damien
Sally Trench
Chad Varah
Mother Teresa
Dr Barnardo
Don Bosco
Terry Waite

You may have heard of other Christians who are in the news currently, and whom you think to be good examples of Christian values in action. Feel free to choose someone who interests you and whom you can find out more about.

Extension work

A

Display your work in the classroom, or *present* it as part of a school assembly.

B

There may be people in your local community, your parish or local church, or in your street or neighbourhood, not necessarily of the Christian faith, but whose work in the community is inspired by religious faith and values. *Invite* them and the school to share their story with your class.

Tasks 18–20

1. *How did you organise your work on Christian values? Were you successful in finding out what Christians value?*
2. *Which person did you study in your project? What did you learn from your work?*
3. *Did you do any extension work? Which?*

Review of the module

Which parts of this module did you most enjoy working on?

Which parts did you feel you did your best work on?

What is the most important thing you have learned from your study of Values Level One?

How do you think this module could be improved? Was there anything which you feel would have made the module more interesting?

On the whole, was your work in this module better than in previous ones?

How did we do?

We are the Champions!

Managing your own learning

Were you

1. Usually on time for class/usually late for class?
2. Hardworking . . . most of the time/some of the time/not very often?
3. Able to work by yourself sometimes?
4. Able to work with others in a group?

Did you

5. Find the work very easy or very difficult?
6. Work when the teacher was busy with other people or only when the teacher was with you?
7. Cooperate with the teacher?
8. Did you follow up any of the work you did at home by reading or finding out more about any of the topics you have covered?
9. Did you do any extension/project work?

Do you

10. Find it easy to tell the teacher of any problems you had?
11. Prefer to work by yourself or with others?

Now, share what you have done with your class teacher.

Congratulations! **You have completed this Level One module on *Values*.**

You can be proud of your work and *value it*!